P.

0|'|'   peace ☮ ♡ ♡

Aymee

Fourth Edition

Cover Design by Moenja Schijven

HAPPINESS FOR HUMANKIND PLAYBOOK:

Sustainable Happiness in 5 Steps

by Dr. Aymee Coget

Sustainable Happiness Expert

Founder of the Five Step Formula to Sustainable Happiness

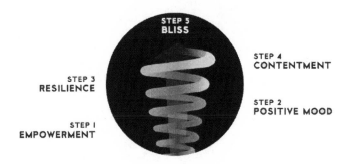

STEP 5
BLISS

STEP 4
CONTENTMENT

STEP 3
RESILIENCE

STEP 2
POSITIVE MOOD

STEP 1
EMPOWERMENT

Put happiness science to work for you!

Dedication

This book is dedicated to my family, friends, teachers, students, and business partners, all of whom have taught me the wisdom which is compiled in the following pages. I am grateful for the opportunity to realize my true spiritual calling and to be fueled with endless energy for the cause of helping millions of people live happier lives.

Walter E. Jacobson, MD
Diplomate, American Board of Psychiatry & Neurology
18300 Roscoe Blvd, IFL Tower, 4th Floor
Northridge, California 91328
(818) 885-8500, ext. 3724
(818) 727-1451 (fax)
walterdoc@mac.com

September 18, 2009

Dear Aymee,

I want to formally congratulate you on putting together a sustainable life improvement program, your "Happiness Makeover," that is extremely effective.

It is the transformative regimen that you teach and coach in the consultation sessions that gives people cognitive-behavioral tools and mind-body-spirit routines which, if they practice consistently, daily, will take them on a path of self-discovery and growth, the by-products of which are sustainable happiness and inner peace.

Your curriculum is, indeed, an excellent one. During the three months of my own Happiness Makeover, I found myself truly becoming happier. I felt more energized and motivated to pursue my life goals.

More valuable than that, the experience helped me to clarify my life goals, in the sense that your program encourages people to look at core strengths and values, and it encourages people to discover their authenticity, to become the fullness of who they are.

I find myself now, after a month out of the program, continuing to enjoy the benefits of the program. My attitude about life, work, and people, has improved. I see my life as an adventure unfolding, which is exciting, especially compared to my previous feeling about my life which was "It's pretty good, could be better, getting through it."

As you can see, I am an extremely satisfied customer. Thank you.

Sincerely,

Walter E. Jacobson, MD

"*This book by Dr. Aymee Coget is a giant step forward for anyone wanting to raise their deep, inner contentment levels to a solid TEN. Her **5 Steps are easy to use**, they work, and are wonderful for helping anyone become happier. She has my unqualified support.*"
- *Bob Nozik, MD, author of "Happy 4 Life: Here's How to Do It" and "Happy Tymes Rhymes: Just for the Fun of It"*

"*This book is phenomenal and **life changing**! This book is an amazing piece! Perhaps the missing key to happiness does lie deep in our hearts!*"
- *Mike Otoma, College Student, Kenya*

"*These 5 steps brought me to sustainable happiness, and they will bring you to sustainable happiness too! All you have to do is **follow the steps, and you can be content and fulfilled** even when obstacles are placed in your way!*" - *T.T., San Francisco, CA*

"*The lessons in this book is the most **realistic approach** to happiness I have yet to see .*" - *N.A., San Francisco, CA*

"*Anyone seeking to put happiness into their own hands would benefit from working with Dr. Aymee and Happiness for HumanKind.*"
- *Dr. Marshall Goldsmith, #1 Leadership Thinker, Exec Coach, NYT Bestselling Author. Dartmouth Tuck Professor Mgmt Practice*

"*Dr. Aymee Coget is one of the most wonderfully passionate people I've ever met. She is exuberant, fun, serious about results and very committed. I thoroughly enjoyed my time with her and found her Happiness Makeover® program to be **extremely valuable**. I loved the integration of spiritual healing with practical exercises; a few of which touched me very deeply. Aymee was an Angel of sorts during a very challenging period in my life. I am very grateful for her personally and for her commitment to happiness and goodness on this Earth.*"
- *R.H., Healthcare CEO*

"*Dr. Aymee is the personification of her work: in addition to being an expert in Positive Psychology and Sustainable Happiness, who effectively teaches others how to discover their own happiness and unlimited creative potential, she is someone who exudes happiness, positivity, enthusiasm and self-confidence on a daily basis. There is no doubt she practices what she preaches. My experience as a student of her Happiness Makeover® was **empowering and transformative**. She is truly gifted and I highly recommend her.*" - Walter Jacobson, MD, Diplomat of the American Psychiatric Association, Los Angeles, CA

"*I came into the Happiness Makeover® lost, stressed, and depressed. I learned not only that happiness and peace come from within, but also the skills needed to achieve these conditions. I left with a profound appreciation of the beauty that pervades myself and life in general, and I am excited, confident, and assured in my quest to actualize the life path that is true to myself. and **I am of course HAPPY!**"*
- R. M., Healthcare Consultant, San Francisco, CA

"*I currently hold a Master of Public Health degree from the university of Michigan and am certified as a Holistic Health coach from the Institute for Integrative Nutrition. My experience in the Happiness Makeover® has been nothing short of life changing and I continue to build confidence using the tools I have learned to achieve a lifetime of bliss. I give two big thumbs up to the field of positive psychology because it makes so much more sense than the "medical model" of psychology - the idea that **you can create happiness in any and every moment** is so much more empowering than rehashing past hurts and trauma. I fell in love with the idea of sustainable happiness and positive psychology the first time I spoke with Dr. Aymee. Without much hesitation, I signed up for the Happiness Makeover®, and a few weeks thereafter, I decided that enrolling in the Happiness Coach training program was the obvious next step for me. After completing the program in the Summer of 2012, I hope to work with others who've been particularly affected and consumed by stress and anxiety in their daily lives.*"
- A. G., Researcher, Baltimore, MD

Contents

CHAPTER 5: CONTENTMENT

CHAPTER 6: BLISS

CHAPTER 7: SUSTAINABLE HAPPINESS

CHAPTER 8: INTEGRATIVE APPROACH

CHAPTER 9: TRANSFORMATION

INTRODUCTION

Are you ready to be happy?

I promise you have the power to be happy, and I have developed a five step program that will show you how to enjoy every moment of every day, to find a deep and lasting sense of peace and contentment.

You will still experience fear and anger, yet I am going to show you how you can learn to live in the upward spiral instead of the downward spiral.

We all know and understand the downward spiral. The truth is, happiness is life or death. It is easy to dismiss happiness like it is a fluffy topic unworthy of discussion, something to ignore, or sweep under the rug. Happiness is such a personal topic that it is impossible to have a real conversation about it, unless you are talking to a trained professional behind four closed walls with a confidentiality agreement.

We live in a world where we are protected from meaningful, emotional experiences by being polite. While technological advances like cellular telephones and email have given us more opportunities to communicate with each other, it is harder to truly connect with people.

We are taught etiquette demands the "How are you?" "I am good." Plastic Exchange

People lie about their happiness and fake their happiness all day every day. We are bombarded by messages in media and advertising that promise happiness by rewarding ourselves with soft drinks, cheeseburgers, jewelry, cars, cosmetics, clothes - we see something, we seek it, we obtain it, we enjoy it, yet the allure fades as soon as our attention is stolen by the next big thing. Sustainable happiness never comes from sports cars or designer clothes; it comes from the awareness that we are OK just as we are.

In 2010, scientists found the brain changes when certain activities are performed. We have the ability to mold our brains every day! Once you learn how to be happy, you will create an operating system for your brain so that being happy becomes automatic.

When people use the techniques that are based in the new science of happiness, positive mood increases, resiliency increases, and contentment settles in. States of bliss and joy are achieved!

You need to feel empowered to take leadership of your happiness. If you wait around for someone else or something else to make you happy, you will be left empty, unfulfilled and discontent. Zero people or things external to yourself can make you happy forever.

Your happiness is your responsibility.

You have the ability to choose how to respond to everything that happens to you. The five steps of the upward spiral provide a scientifically proven method for giving you total control of your mood.

At some point, this is a choice in everyone's life.

Most people are looking for an answer. According to the National Institute of Health, depressed people seek out on average three to five types of treatment.

People are looking for answers, spending money, getting shock therapy, taking trips to India to find the pearl of eternal contentment and pure bliss.

The real answer is...

Follow your heart.

I know it sounds cheesy, yet your true contentment and bliss are available to you through engaging and listening to your heart's guidance.

This is an inner guidance system that will truly lead each individual to lasting contentment and frequent states of bliss. The trick is in learning to listen to your authentic self rather than buying into the idea that happiness is something to be attained when you (fill in the blank).

You can choose to be happy
about anything, at any time, under any circumstance.

Many of us cling to emotional patterns we learned when we were young. You may have been mistreated or neglected which caused you to react by carrying pain; that trauma is carried into other problems in the way we relate to others. In the immortal words of Sheryl Crow, "It's not getting what you want, it's wanting what you've got."

Before that is even able to be accessed, there has to be empowerment. There has to be a willingness to acknowledge that the *other* way is inadequate. Ownership with the attitude of wanting to do something about it, a desire to work for a frequent positive mood, and resiliency - these are prerequisites before one can achieve lasting contentment.

I am warning you, this is a process, and the five steps introduced here are sequential. Then they become unidimensional meaning you adopt all five steps all of the time.

Be gentle with yourself, yet strive to follow as much of the program as you can fit into your life. The more you incorporate these ideas into your life, the more you will enjoy your life.

You will be happy.

In my avant-garde Leadership Training program, the Happiness Makeover™, clients undergo an intense immersion experience while implementing a specific process which requires a lot of work, finesse, activity, exercise, and awareness.

It incorporates:

1. A leadership approach to take charge of one's happiness
2. Cutting edge advancements in happiness research for daily routine systems
3. Wisdom from mentors who have achieved sustainable happiness for decades
4. Accessing one's heart's voice for deep questions like "Who am I?" and "What is my life's purpose?"
5. A 90-day nutritional molecular cleanse (optional weight loss) and brain chemistry balancing
6. Daily exercise
7. Three Reiki attunements (healing the heart, emotional healing, and healing the soul) and three energy healings which heal past traumas through chakra cleansing.

Using an integral approach of mind-body-spirit is what it has taken to help people develop deep inner contentment as well as achieve states of bliss and joy in a reasonably quick time frame of ninety days.

You as a reader will be on your own to incorporate the body and spirit techniques that I describe at the end of the book. Most of this book addresses the mental skills required to obtain sustainable happiness once and for all which accounts for the mind component of the Happiness Makeover®.

The techniques taught in this book *will work* for you if you do them.

The trick to anything is *take action.*

Knowing this information and using this information are two different things so I want to encourage you to bring your A game to your happiness. This is the Olympic team for happiness! Remember that class you loved so much? The one you ate, slept, drank, and dreamt? The one that challenged you yet was the most rewarding?

Your A game and your Olympic athlete mindset
are what you will have to bring to
master your Happiness Program.

The time is NOW.

Think about this leadership training program as a car wash. There are different tools at different places, yet when used systematically, each car (regardless of which type or how dirty) becomes shiny and clean at the end.

People look for an answer when they are down, broken, in pain, stressed out, or even suicidal.

These five steps will teach you
what you need to know
to stop the downward spiral,
get off the emotional roller coaster, and
create your upward spiral
once and for all!

CHAPTER 1: GETTING STARTED

WHY CARE ABOUT YOUR HAPPINESS?

In 2005, there was a meta analysis research study which combined all of the studies indicating benefits received by people who have achieved frequent positive affect. In other words, they sustained their happiness. This is a 54-page document of empirically-based benefits received by happy people. It shows that happy people have it better in a lot of different ways.

In fact, if you analyze the brain of a happy person versus the brain of an unhappy person, the brain of the happy person is much more flexible, enlightened, and dynamic. You also can easily *see* the difference between a brain image of a happy person versus that of an unhappy person.

Besides the brain alone, happy people have benefits in health, make more money, get promoted more often, have better relationships, and generally live seven years longer.

Everything is better when you are happy.

If people are given the choice between being happy or being unhappy, people will choose to be happy. Now, because of the science of happiness you can learn how to be happy just like you learned basic math.

If you apply all the lessons here, you will have your happiness in your own hands!

This is one of the most freeing things you can do for yourself.

Without the tools outlined for you in this book, your life is like a roller coaster: up and down, up and down. If good things are happening, you are happy, and if bad things are happening, you are unhappy. Yet, if you use the program I introduce, then your life will naturally skyrocket out of the dizzying roller coaster of life into an intergalactic upward spiral of peace, contentment, and joy!

When you are in this upward spiral, you experience the benefits received by happy people which are better health, making more money, recovering from illness faster, getting promoted more often, having better, longer lasting relationships, and living longer.

Does your happiness seem worth the work?

WHAT IS HAPPINESS?

Happiness can fall under the umbrella of empowerment, positive mood, positive emotion, resiliency, deep inner contentment, a sense of fulfillment, and even bliss or joy. The best way to understand it is through types of happiness.

There are three types of happiness:

HEDONIC HAPPINESS

It is derived from hedonism, something good happens and you are happy. 100% of people have experienced this type of happiness. When I tell people I am a sustainable happiness expert, a lot of times people seem to think I am seeking to sustain the positive emotion of happiness (which is impossible to sustain because of the nature of emotions). This type of happiness will come and go. When things are good, you are going to be happy, and when things are bad, you will be unhappy. Your emotional well-being becomes a leaf in the wind to whatever your circumstances are in any given moment. You can be promoted in your job and be elated, and the next thing you know, you are in rush hour traffic with your mother-in-law yelling at you on the phone. Your happiness is long gone. You find yourself on the hedonic treadmill, always in pursuit of something outside of yourself in the form of the right person, place, thing, or circumstance.

American culture focuses on teaching an achievement strategy for happiness, driving you to obtain the right person, place, thing, and circumstance so THEN you will be happy. This is a mirage, a false illusion. If you think you will be happy when you get all the right things in your life just the way you want them, you are using a failed strategy when it comes to lasting contentment. In 2006, science showed that when you do get the right things, people, and circumstances in your life you will become unhappy within three months. This is because of hedonic adaptation. This means you adapt to your circumstances and want change. This leaves you jumping back on the hedonic treadmill, in a constant mode of seeking without ever being satisfied, and consistently feeling depressed, stressed, unfulfilled, and discontent.

I need to ask you to change your strategy

when it comes to achieving sustainable happiness.

Obviously, your hedonic strategy will probably fail. You may have already seen other people who have it all, and they are still unhappy. *You* may have it all and still be unhappy. I want to inspire you to choose the methods of achieving deep inner contentment and a sense of fulfillment that are outlined in this book instead of seeking the answers through your external world.

EUDAIMONIC HAPPINESS

Aristotle introduced this type of happiness. EU- means good, DAIMON is spirit, -IC is nature of; put it together, and you get the nature of a good spirit (which you truly have!). It is the nature of our humanity to want to feel good all the time. Even though this concept was introduced in Ancient Greece, American psychology only caught up in the early 2,000s. There are four things which need to be in place in order to unlock this type of happiness. I use the acronym MAPS - Meaning, Authenticity, Purpose, and Strengths. When you have meaning and purpose in your life, when you are in touch with your authentic self, and you are using your strengths, you are indeed happier. In fact, you are fulfilled and content. This is a different type of happiness than hedonic happiness. Hedonic happiness is *feeling* happy whereas eudaimonic happiness is *being* happy. You are being happy because you are engaged in your MAPS. Instead of seeking to get the right person, place, thing, and circumstance in your life, you seek to fulfill your MAPS. Follow the truth in your heart to discover meaning, authenticity, purpose, and strengths in your life. When you have actualized your MAPS, then you will feel eudaimonia which is sustainable.

Eudaimonia can still be experienced at the same time as negative emotional experiences. I can still be engaged in my MAPS yet grieve the loss of a loved one, for example. This is where you accept your human experience and master your emotional experience, choosing to manage your emotional state to whatever is appropriate in the moment.

CHAIRONIC HAPPINESS

This is spiritual joy and bliss. You may have gone to church or some meditation retreat or a spiritual place where you saw people in amazing states of bliss and joy with their eyes rolling back in their head. They seemed blissed out to the point where they look like they belong in a museum. How many people really walk around with this type of bliss and joy with consistency? This type of bliss and joy comes from the connection to something greater than yourself whether you want to call it God, the universe, or whatever it is to you.

The best way to understand these types of happiness is through the source of happiness. The source of hedonic happiness is something external to you, the source of eudaimonic happiness is your heart based MAPS, and the source of chaironic happiness is a connection to something greater than yourself.

POSITIVE PSYCHOLOGY

It started with Dr. Martin Seligman at the University of Pennsylvania who is a former American Psychological Association President. He was in his garden with his five-year-old daughter, and she looked at him and said, "Daddy, why are you such a grump?" He reflected on what his daughter said and thought, "Yeah, why am I such a grump?" He realized that in his entire career he was studying depression instead of happiness, so he went into the research and found there was a ratio of 17:1 depression to happiness studies in psychology. He also realized that since the 1940s, funding institutions would only fund research that fixed problems. Academics are smart people so they created all kinds of problems to fix, and now we have the DSM which is the current Diagnostic Manual for Psychological Disorders.

Recognizing the need for change, in 1998 Dr. Seligman introduced positive psychology as an exciting new field of psychology where the focus was placed on the positive experience of life instead of fixing problems. Funding was awarded to research focusing on positive emotions, happiness, love, forgiveness, creativity, and all of these wonderful positive emotional experiences. The field of happiness has made greater advances in the last ten years than in the last 200. Since there has been such amazing new knowledge in this field of mental health, I have discovered a way to teach happiness like math in five steps.

This is a miracle!

A MAJOR SCIENTIFIC SHIFT!

Every single person needs to know it.

Regardless of any diagnosis such as depression, anxiety, bipolar disorder, obsessive compulsive disorder, or even schizophrenia, you can learn these concepts and become happier.

WHAT IS THE HAPPINESS MAKEOVER®?

This leadership training program is undergoing study by university professors, was mentioned in the *New York Times* in 2007, and is endorsed by a diplomat of the American Psychiatry Association all because it is helping people achieve bliss after years of depression and stress.

This training teaches how to adopt a practice based in happiness science so you can use it throughout your daily life.

The makeover incorporates positive psychology practice every day, day in and day out for ninety days straight; it also moves beyond positive psychology by incorporating an integral approach to address the needs of the body and spirit.

It is a leading edge, mind-body-spirit training program.

Mind - Positive Psychology/5 Steps to Sustainable Happiness

Body - Nutritional Cleansing Technology/Daily Exercise

10

Spirit - Reiki Energy Attunements/Healings

The mind focuses on adopting five steps to achieving sustainable happiness which is:

1. Empowerment - making The Happiness Decision
2. Positive mood - using happiness boosting techniques
3. Resiliency - using tools when coping with happiness challenges
4. Contentment - developing meaning and purpose in your life, being your true authentic self, using your strengths, and
5. Bliss - having faith when faced with the unknown.

It also includes a ninety-day usage of Isagenix nutrition technology to balance brain chemistry, provide optimal nutrition, and remove toxicity from the body. Clients also adhere to a daily exercise regimen. The spirit portion is satisfied by Reiki energy attunements and healings where the client undergoes three different 21-day chakra cleanses (one per month) focusing on healing the heart, emotional healing, and healing the soul. Subconscious issues of survival, security, self-esteem, love, communication, intuition, and spirituality are healed during the chakra cleanses.

As the body and spirit components are gently in the background of the makeover, the forefront focuses on learning how to be happy like math: step by step, every day in every way.

How many people do you know who understand 2+2? Honestly, more people know 2+2 than those who are literate. If we can teach happiness like we teach math, every single person on the face of the Earth needs to know how to do it. We have been unable to teach happiness before because we were without the science of happiness. We have made great advances in the area of happiness in the last several years, and it is extremely important that you benefit by incorporating happiness science in your day to day life experience.

The Happiness Makeover™ teaches you simply how to do it step by step. All lessons take a maximum of five steps: five steps to achieving sustainable happiness, five steps for living the moment, five steps to overcoming adversity, and four steps in achieving an inner feeling of contentment.

This program works! I am excited for you!

SUSTAINABLE HAPPINESS IN 5 STEPS

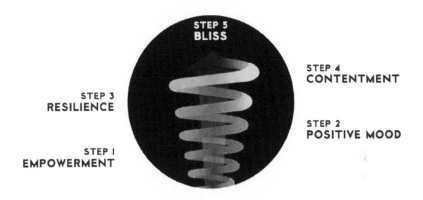

These five steps will bring your life into an upward spiral.

Once you know how to implement all of the lessons I teach, you will achieve an upward spiral in your life.

Using positive psychology helps create the upward spiral.

I know many of you have heard of the downward spiral.

This is the upward spiral.

I fondly call it magic and rainbows.

Magic and rainbows is an experience in life where you achieve synchronistic flow in your daily life, and everything goes your way. You always get the parking spot when you pull in front of a busy restaurant, your friend picks up the phone when you really need to talk, you receive the promotion at work, you make more money than ever before, you have more fulfilling relationships, you are healthy, and you are the one who is sharing your joy with others. This magic and rainbows experience in life is what you have likely strived for and never achieved. This failure is because you are likely constantly disappointed with life, frustrated at your circumstances, angry at the world and everything in it, never living in the moment, obsessed with achievement, thinking negatively, and desperate for change. Yet the only thing you know is the emotional roller coaster of life.

Or even worse- the downward spiral.

The five steps outlined in this book will teach you wisdom from people who have achieved sustainable happiness in their lives for decades in addition to the science of happiness, positive psychology.

The methods taught in this book have given proven results over and over.

The purpose of this book is to show you how to end the up and down emotional roller coaster as well as eliminate the possibility of a downward spiral from ever occurring for the rest of your life!

How am I going to do that?

I am going to teach you how to be happy.

You see, it was never your fault that you are experiencing the roller coaster or the downward spiral. The upward spiral had yet to be even introduced or discovered until 2004!

In 2005, there was a study that showed all of the benefits for happy people. These benefits are the magic and rainbows to which I refer. Then in 2008, positive emotional interventions were released that showed if we do simple things like acts of kindness, we will become happier. In 2010, research showed that changes do occur in the brain when one performs positive interventions for a short period of time while treating symptoms of depression, bipolar disorder, and even schizophrenia. I would be willing to speculate that this would even decrease stress, aid in treating ADHD, save marriages, heal illness, and perform miracles. In 2012, research showed there are differing types of happiness and the effects of each type on our lives.

My point: this information is cutting edge, effective, and when implemented in the right ways, can better our lives tenfold.

I had tea with Dr. Ryan Howell, a Happiness Professor at San Francisco State University, and we talked about the connection between the theory and practice of happiness.

He joked and said,

"I would hate to put the secret to happiness in a 140 character tweet."

He looked shocked when I said,

"Really? I have it down to five steps."

This researcher is currently investigating my client base since I have piqued his curiosity with my confidence, clarity, simplicity, and most importantly, results.

These five steps of achieving sustainable happiness

are the yellow brick road to achieving

magic and rainbows in your life.

Does that sound good?

Yes, positive psychology shows a 3:1 ratio of positive to negative emotional experiences will give you an upward spiral. If you truly harness the power of the positive emotional experience throughout your life, you will see great things unfold moment to moment.

Let's start!

1. Empowerment - Happiness Decision

2. Positive Mood - Happiness Boosters

3. Resiliency - Happiness Challenges

4. Contentment - Heart Based MAPS (meaning, authenticity, purpose, and strengths)

5. Bliss - Faith

The Happiness Makeover® training program deliverables include: empowerment over your own happiness, how to create a positive mood whenever you want, resiliency by overcoming life's challenges, deep inner contentment and a sense of fulfillment, and states of bliss and joy!

If you are interested in creating more of these things in your life, then doing this work is worth your while.

Yes, it is work.

You have to put time and attention on your happiness instead of waiting around for it to happen to you.

1. Empowerment - Make The Happiness Decision

First and foremost, you have to take the initiative to decide to be happy. Before you do anything, you make a decision to do it. Before you attend school, you decide to attend school. Before you get married, you decide to get married. Before you take a shower, you decide to take a shower. Before you do the dishes, you decide to do the dishes. Same with happiness - you have to decide to do something different. You have to decide to take your happiness into your own hands. That is the very first step.

2. Positive Mood - Use Happiness Boosters

It is imperative that you create a happiness practice filled with happiness boosters in your day to day experience. A happiness booster is any scientific or practical method that will increase your happiness at any given time, and, therefore, will boost your mood whenever you want. These are things like kindness, gratitude, smiling, laughing, living in the moment, and positive thinking. I know it is easier said than done which is why there is a lesson here on each particular happiness booster. My clients are on a formula of happiness boosters with a morning routine, a daytime routine, and a sleep routine. They create a new daily happiness practice through adopting a routine system based on happiness science. Monitoring these different boosting techniques is very beneficial to see which ones really work for you. If you stop testing these happiness boosters, you are going to be dependent on the outside world to boost your mood whenever the outside world feels like it. There is a better way to live!

3. Resiliency - Overcome Happiness Challenges

Of course, if you are choosing happiness and you are doing your happiness boosters, you will still experience difficult emotional situations. It is vital that you have these tools so you can maintain your happiness even in the face of adversity. What differentiates human beings from animals is that we can think so you can choose to respond to any given situation instead of react to it. The tools taught to cope with happiness challenges will help ensure your upward spiral keeps going up. These tools are things like acceptance, forgiveness, and seeing the good in the bad. This is so you can keep your cool, calm, and collected state when dealing with each challenge. I recognize that you may have trouble being happy about your challenges. You can choose happiness *and* handle the situation at hand with a clear brain which builds resilience.

4. Contentment - Follow your heart's MAPS

Contentment and fulfillment are feelings in your heart. It is the opposite of feeling empty inside. Did you know there is a difference between your heart and mind? It is important you engage your heart when it comes to things like meaning, authenticity, purpose, and strengths in your life, and this is why I call it your Heart Based MAPS (MAPS is an acronym for meaning, authenticity, purpose, and strengths). Unhappy people are likely to have a lack of meaning and purpose in their lives. They are likely to be totally out of touch with their authentic self, and they are seeking to fix their problems instead of using their strengths. It is essential for you to foster these MAPS from your heart instead of your mind as it will help you achieve deep inner contentment, a sense of fulfillment, and peace of mind.

5. Bliss - Faith

Faith means trust. Trust if you put out positive you get back positive. Trust yourself to achieve a realistic goal with an achievable plan and believe in yourself along the way. Faith is a connection to something greater than yourself where you can achieve states of bliss and joy.

I recommend you learn these five steps like you learned 2+2. I suggest you bring your Olympian student attitude and give your best to mastering each lesson. What is more important than your own happiness anyway?

When you have mastered these steps,

you will achieve sustainable happiness in your life.

You will see your upward spiral with your own eyes, and you will be shocked to see how it will bring magic and rainbows into every area of your life!

CHAPTER 2: EMPOWERMENT

STEP 1 - MAKE YOUR HAPPINESS DECISION

The first step in feeling better right now is making The Happiness Decision, choosing happiness. Every single one of my mentors and positive psychology experts agree that the first step is your happiness decision. This means you have to take your happiness into your own hands.

You can choose to stop sitting around and waiting for a person, place, thing, or circumstance to make you happy.

The only person responsible for your happiness is yourself.

Taking your happiness into your own hands is the most freeing thing you can do for yourself in your journey toward feeling better and learning how to be happy.

As an inspiration, we have Lionel Ketchian who has read over 2,500 books on happiness. He is the founder of the Happiness Clubs Worldwide and one of my mentors. He wrote a declaration called The Happiness Decision which is a certificate you can sign.

This is the most important decision of your life!

Go to the mirror, look at yourself deep in the eyes, put your hand on your heart, and get ready.

This is a lot more important than taking a shower and doing the dishes. This is the crux of your well-being.

I am so proud of you for getting yourself into this moment and taking charge of your happiness.

Without further adieu, here we go. Repeat after me: "I, _____ do solemnly decide to adopt The Happiness Decision by being happy now. Rather than react to my problems, I will use happiness to respond to them. Forsaking all negative thoughts. Regardless of circumstances, in all ways I will choose happiness for the rest of my sweet life."

CONGRATULATIONS!

HIGH FIVE!

BIG HUG!

Print out The Happiness Decision Declaration, sign it in red ink, and put it on your refrigerator. The skill in upholding this happiness decision is in forsaking all negative thoughts and responding to circumstances with happiness. These two intentions will require a great amount of work in order to be able to follow through with your intention to make The Happiness Decision today and every day for the rest of your life.

The Happiness Decision

I, _____

**Do solemnly Decide
to adopt the Happiness Decision
by BEING HAPPY NOW**

**Rather than react to my problems
I will use Happiness to Respond to them
forsaking all negative thoughts.**

**Regardless of circumstances,
IN ALL WAYS I WILL Choose Happiness
for the rest of MY LIFE.**

Signed _____

Date _____

www.happinessclub.com

This happiness decision is very multi-dimensional.

It seems simple, yet there is a lot behind it.

To understand the complexity behind making The Happiness Decision, I offer this exercise to you.

1. Start by printing Dr. Bob's Happiness Decision Nuggets below.
2. Find and watch Lionel's YouTube presentation on "Making The Happiness Decision" (search online for "Lionel Ketchian Happiness Decision").

Dr. Bob Nozik is one of my close mentors. Many years ago, I introduced Dr. Bob to Lionel, and Dr. Bob became fascinated by how Lionel could in fact sustain his happiness for that long simply by making the decision. Dr. Bob has also been happy for more than 25 years straight, and he wrote a book which I use in the Happiness Makeover® program. It is called "Happy 4 Life: Here's How to Do It". I highly recommend this book because it is written by a sustainably happy person. Dr. Bob took twenty years to develop his 25-year sustained happiness through his twelve keys whereas Lionel took 24 hours to develop his 27-year sustained happiness based on the simple decision. Dr. Bob watched Lionel's presentation, and he wrote down the important points Lionel addresses during his 27-minute monologue. He discusses things like how to be happy if your father is in the hospital, how to be happy in a family argument, and what it really, truly means to make this happiness decision.

Your homework is to print out Dr. Bob's Happiness Decision Nuggets and watch Lionel Ketchian's presentation on The Happiness Decision. Make a checkmark next to every Decision Nugget as you watch.

When you complete this exercise, I will feel confident you will know what it means to make The Happiness Decision once and for all!

You have made the very first step you need in order to feel better now.

Dr. Bob's Happiness Decision Nuggets

Making The Happiness Decision with Lionel Ketchian

(Introduction by George Ortega)

1. Lionel's Epiphany: 1990, Christmas Eve
2. Note: holiday depression common.
3. Society gives OK to be happy on Christmas Eve...so he became aware of being happy.
4. Yet happiness comes and goes; he understood it was fleeting. It is insane being happy all the time; it will go away.
5. Well, he thought, what could be so important for him to give his happiness away?
6. His happiness led him to feel gratitude and compassion. (Tipping the service station attendant who did good work...the attendant was happy yet it was Lionel who felt great afterwards; felt really, REALLY happy!)
7. He then realized that losing his happiness now would be a really big loss; what would be worth that? His happiness felt so great so it would have to be something really, really important.
8. Many are unfamiliar with what real happiness feels like, yet everyone knows what unhappiness is like.
9. We never lose our happiness; to lose it, we must give it away. (Lionel's example of later Christmas Eve, conflict regarding cars at home. He discovered he could lose the argument, let go of the drama, and keep his happiness!)
10. Life will keep testing you...tempting you to give away your happiness.
11. Happiness, more than an emotion, is a life strategy—there is great power in this realization.
12. Practice preventing difficult life circumstances taking your happiness—the only way they can is if you give it away.
13. Being right is never worth giving away your happiness.
14. There is a difference between intellectually knowing about (we have known about happiness since Aristotle 2,600 years ago) and actually experiencing happiness.
15. Even severe life circumstances out of your control are never worth giving away your happiness (for example, Lionel's dad's acute M.I. - in fact, his happiness seemed to help).

16. Giving away your happiness over anything out of your control is insanity; even when the world says it is OK.
17. Giving your happiness to others is different, and this enhances your happiness.
18. There is a positive connection between health and happiness (now scientifically verified) as well as a negative correlation between health and unhappiness (stress and disease).
19. You can be happy and still have problems, even major ones; we all have problems; life is all about problems.
20. You are/can be separate from your problems. When you see the truth of this you can be happy even in the midst of these problems.
21. Acceptance is the way out for those problems out of your control.
22. This means you can still work on improving life and getting rid of problems. Those who are happy, in fact, have more energy for working on the problems they can work to improve.
23. You choose happiness moment by moment, hour by hour, day by day. Whatever comes up, you can ask yourself if it is worth losing your happiness for it...and will that help? It is a present moment choice all the time being happy in the moment, moment by moment.
24. When you are happy you make better decisions; your mind is clearer and more creative.
25. Happy people are more fun to be with, more attractive to others, have better long term relationships, are healthier, and live longer.

If you are still having a hard time making The Happiness Decision, I understand. It seems pretty simple minded to think if we could just choose to be happy it would end all problems and suffering.

For a moment, think about someone other than yourself. Think about your family, your neighbors, or your colleagues at work. Think about the human population.

Think about the change you want to see in the world. I would bet you would want others to be happy. I bet you want peace on earth. If we have peace on earth, then you would agree with me that we would have paradise on earth. People would be laughing and smiling.

Let's start with you making your happiness decision right now; otherwise, you are contributing to the world's misery.

This happiness decision is going to influence up to three degrees of separation of every single person you come into contact with, according to Harvard research in 2008. If you are having a hard time choosing happiness for yourself, choose happiness for your loved ones, colleagues, and neighbors. Choose happiness because it is your first step in creating peace on earth.

making this decision

and

sustaining this decision

are two totally different things.

Now that you have made this happiness decision, you have to think about how to sustain it, and we do that through mastering the following four steps.

TIMING FOR STEP 1

The desire to make The Happiness Decision is a prerequisite to making The Happiness Decision. If you are having a hard time making this step, I recommend watching Lionel's Happiness Decision video to gain further understanding of exactly what it means to take your happiness into your own hands.

Print, Sign, and Post The Happiness Decision = 3 minutes

Watch Lionel's 27-minute presentation on making The Happiness Decision while making checks next to each of Dr. Bob's Happiness Decision Nuggets = 27 minutes

TOTAL AMOUNT OF TIME FOR STEP 1 = 30 minutes

STEP 1 MASTERY

You know you have mastered step one when you are constantly faced with adversity and choose to be happy anyway. You know you are in a level of mastery when bad moods, stress, and anxiety are a thing of the past. When you realize zero person or thing can take your happiness away from you, you have mastered your happiness decision.

When you have forsaken all negative thoughts

and are responding to circumstances with happiness

is when you have mastered your happiness decision.

CHAPTER 3: POSITIVE MOOD

STEP 2 - USE HAPPINESS BOOSTERS

ADOPT A HAPPINESS PRACTICE

You may already have a yoga practice, an exercise practice, a healthy eating practice, a practice visiting your family, or whatever it may be. You do it as a regular experience. You have to do the same thing with happiness. You must build in a happiness routine every day.

Until now, happiness has been a byproduct of other things in your life. You have been getting your happiness from a specific person, place, thing, or circumstance when things go your way. However, life certainly goes in directions other than *your way* which puts your happiness in the hands of everything and everyone else.

Creating a happiness practice in your life allows you to cut the cord between everything and your happiness. Go ahead and think about it for a second. Think about how freeing it is going to be when zero people or things are in charge of your happiness.

What I am talking about when I say to create a happiness practice is

use happiness boosters

every morning, every day, and every night.

It is true! If you can fit in five minutes of happiness boosting techniques in the morning, use them throughout the day as well as before you go to sleep, you will generally feel happier in life.

Remember, this idea of feeling happier in life is really beneficial to you because there are so many scientifically proven benefits for people who have achieved frequent positive mood.

Creating happiness practices in your life is going to generate a frequent feeling of positive well-being and positive mood which will lead you to what positive psychology calls the "upward spiral".

Employing positive psychology techniques will help you build this upward spiral into your life because you will implement a consistent, positive emotional experience. This is only to the point where you have a minimum of three positive emotional experiences to every one negative emotional experience (the 3:1 upward spiral ratio mentioned in Chapter 2).

Personally, I would say how about a ratio of fifteen to zero?

My hypothesis is that my clients get a minimum of 10:1 ratio! That is a conservative estimate.

At the very minimum, and shooting for a realistic goal, let's go for a three to one positive to negative emotional experience in your day to day living.

Introducing the upward spiral concept is one of the founding papers in positive psychology thanks to Dr. Barbara L. Fredrickson, a professor of psychology, and Dr. Marcial F. Losada, a mathematician. They mathematically showed that if you harness the power of your positive emotional experience, your life will indeed turn into an upward spiral.

THIS IS REMARKABLE AND THEY HAVE WON

MANY DISTINGUISHED AWARDS FOR THIS WORK!

Existing in an upward spiral and creating an upward spiral are different things. If you want to experience the upward spiral, you can through implementing a daily happiness practice.

The proprietary formula of happiness boosting techniques outlined in this book is the same daily happiness practice used in the Makeover. It is made up of different happiness boosting techniques based in science or wisdom from others who have achieved sustainable happiness.

Each of these boosters are outlined individually so you can do them one at a time. At the very least, do one booster. What do you have to lose?

On another note, if you are going to bring your A game, do the whole positive psychology practice program like you mean it!

I know sometimes you just need one booster, yet we want to use these boosting techniques to create a positive mood throughout the day.

I highly recommend that you stop waiting around for happiness as a byproduct from a person, place, thing, or circumstance, and create a daily happiness practice.

This is going to help you create

a positive mood whenever you want.

HAPPINESS DAILY ROUTINES

MORNING ROUTINE

Start your morning with a serotonin boost!

"WAKE UP AND SMILE!"

In the Happiness Makeover™ formula of happiness boosters, wake up and smile is the very first one.

Every morning you literally wake up and smile by putting the corners of your mouth towards your cheekbones.

Go ahead and do it. Stronger, stronger, wider, wider, and with more teeth!

This smile triggers serotonin in the brain simply because of the muscular structure in your face. Your brain is without the faintest idea as to why you are smiling or why you are happy; it only recognizes what is happening in the muscular structure of your face.

Now go ahead and keep practicing. In fact, you can create a smile practice any time you want. If you are walking down the hallway, you can walk and smile. If you are showering, you can shower and smile. If you are doing just about anything, you can do it with a smile. So waking up and smiling is one way to create a smile practice in your life. I know it sounds a bit simple, maybe even a little trite. However, have you ever met a happy person who never smiles? That is why it is important to include a conscious, mindful effort in waking up and smiling.

TODAY IS THE HAPPIEST DAY OF MY LIFE!

Set the intention for today to be the best day of your life. You have to make an intention before you do anything, similar to The Happiness Decision.

"Today is the happiest day of my life!"

The person who told me about this specific intention of "Today is the happiest day of my life" is Dr. Robert Muller. He passed away at the age of 85; may he rest in peace. This man was nominated for nineteen Nobel Peace Prizes. He started two Universities of Peace, one in Costa Rica and one in Japan. It is because of him we had the first World Environment Conference. He was the former Assistant Secretary General of the United Nations for forty years. In his retirement from the United Nations, he wrote a book called "Most of All They Taught Me Happiness". This is a very grand statement. If you were on top of the world for your whole career -knowing what is going on all around the planet in every single country- and then deduce the title of your book in reflection during retirement to be "Most of All They Taught Me Happiness", that is huge.

He told me about the power of intention and the power of "today is the happiest day of my life". He says happiness saved his life in a Nazi death camp. He knew the power of intention before he went in there, and he knew they could take everything away from him except his happiness.

He wrote on the wall every single day "Today is the happiest day of my life."

If that man can say, "Today is the happiest day of my life" in a Nazi death camp, you sure as heck can say, "Today is the happiest day of my life" right now.

Regardless of what is happening, where you are, who you are, you can say, "Today is the happiest day of my life." Because without saying,

"Today is the happiest day of my life," will you ever experience the happiest day of your life? Less likely.

If you want to experience what I call the "happiness bounce back" throughout the day, when someone says, "How are you?" you can say, "Today is the happiest day of my life!" Then they will automatically get excited for you due to the emotional contagion of your happiness.

They are going to be happy for you in your happiness.

People are conditioned to have a reason to be happy so more than likely they will ask you, "Why are you so happy? Why is *today* the happiest day of your life?" This is your Happiness Activist moment when you can say, "Because I am making the *choice* to make it the happiest day of my life! I made The Happiness Decision."

This will be spreading the message that each person is in charge of their own happiness and can have the happiest day of their life, too.

Setting the intention is important to do right after the first happiness booster of waking up and smiling.

These happiness boosters are meant to be routine so you can use them every morning, every day, and every night for the rest of your life.

DUCHENNE SMILE PUSH UPS

The first happiness booster I recommend is to wake up and smile. The second is setting the stage for the day to be the happiest day of your life. Next, I recommend going to the bathroom and brushing your teeth. After you are done, do five Duchenne smile pushups.

Duchenne was a neurologist who studied smiles. He determined what was an authentic smile versus an inauthentic smile. The difference is in the corners of your eyes; if they get all crinkly with the crows' feet activated, then it is an authentic smile.

What is a Duchenne smile pushup?

I created this exercise based in positive memory recollection so you can indeed create a Duchenne smile any time you want.

Let's do it now. Read this slowly like a meditation.

Put both feet on the ground. Take a deep breath.

Put one hand on your heart and one hand on your belly.

Take another deep breath.

Drop your awareness into your heart center,

and focus your attention on the area of your heart.

Focus on creating an all loving, all nurturing, all accepting,

open environment there.

Or imagine the last time you were heading to the airport

to pick up someone you loved and how excited you were.

Create that all loving, all nurturing, all accepting,

open environment in your heart center.

Then allow your heartbeat to come through your chest to the palm of your hand.

When you can feel your heartbeat, go ahead and ask yourself to your heart,

"Show me the happiest moment of my life."

Wait for the response. A memory will surface.

That memory will come to you, and bring that happy memory

into your body like it is right here and now.

Visualize that happy memory being right here and now.

Visualize that happiness in your heart center growing stronger and stronger,

warmer and warmer, fuzzier and fuzzier.

Visualize that feeling moving up your chest, into your neck, through your throat, into your mouth, and out the corners of your lips into a Duchenne smile.

Drop your awareness into your heart center.

Focus your attention in the area of your heart.

Bring that happy memory into your body like it is right here and now.

Visualize the feeling getting stronger and stronger,

warmer and warmer, fuzzier and fuzzier.

Visualize the feeling moving up your chest, into your neck, through your throat, into your mouth, and out the corners of your lips into a Duchenne smile.

Repeat.

Drop your awareness into your heart center.

Focus your attention in the area of your heart.

Bring that happy memory into your body like it is right here and now.

Visualize the feeling getting stronger and stronger,

warmer and warmer, fuzzier and fuzzier.

Visualize the feeling moving up your chest, into your neck, through your throat, into your mouth, and out the corners of your lips into a Duchenne smile.

Two more times. Nice and easy.

Drop your awareness into your heart center.

Focus your attention in the area of your heart.

Bring the happy memory into your body like it is right here and now.

Visualize the feeling getting stronger and stronger,

warmer and warmer, fuzzier and fuzzier.

Visualize the feeling moving up your chest, into your neck, through your throat, into your mouth, and out the corners of your lips into a Duchenne smile.

One more. Slowly.

Drop your awareness into your heart center.

Focus your attention in the area of your heart.

Bring the happy memory into your body like it is right here and now.

Visualize the feeling getting stronger and stronger,

warmer and warmer, fuzzier and fuzzier.

Visualize the feeling moving up your chest, into your neck, through your throat, into your mouth, and out the corners of your lips into a Duchenne smile.

There you have it: five Duchenne smile pushups. You can use that memory or any inspiring memory. Have you ever met a happy person without a smile? This is another aspect of creating a happiness practice which includes a smile practice every single day.

LAUGHTER PRACTICE

You may have heard of laughter yoga. This is a social movement that laughs just because there are so many benefits to laughter.

Have you ever met a happy person who never smiles and laughs?

Smiles and laughter are the brick and mortar of your happiness.

Write down "ha ha ha, ho ho ho, he he he".

Repeat out loud

ha ha ha, ho ho ho, he he he, over and over

until you laugh naturally.

There may be some of you who do this and are unable to stimulate natural laughter. However, this is the whole point - to stimulate natural laughter!

You may find yourself with a straight face going "ha ha ha, ho ho ho, he he he" over and over again without actually stimulating natural laughter; this is when you stop taking yourself so seriously and start laughing at yourself doing the laughter practice.

Let's practice again "ha ha ha, ho ho ho, he he he". One, two, three times.

"That is a knee slapper!"

This requires minimal effort and only a few moments of your time. Simply generating a natural chuckle from repeating "ha ha ha, ho ho ho, he he he" will give you a happiness boost.

Do whatever it takes to laugh, watch a laughter video on YouTube, look at funny pictures, or even get a plush toy 'laughter pet'.

"I AM HAPPY!" JUMPS

You are going to do this five times. Stand up, make sure you are alone, put one hand towards the ceiling, jump up five times, and say "I am happy!" on each jump. One, two, three, go!

I never give anyone too much 'thinking' time when it comes to this exercise. You literally have to stop thinking, get up, and jump!

I know it seems totally bizarre to jump up for joy because you probably have never done it (unless you were a paid actor in a car commercial!). For the most part, we have an absence of jumping for joy in our day to day life. In fact, I have only jumped for joy truly one time in my life; I had an incredible experience which triggered a thrust in my body where I literally jumped in the air with pure joy over and over again.

I was on the side of the street and could care less who saw me. I left all self-consciousness out of the picture. I was so happy!

Expressing pure joy!

It may look strange as we want to judge what it looks like to jump up and say, "I am happy," however, this is a 'zest building technique'.

This allows zest to run through your body, and zest is a character strength in positive psychology that stimulates happiness. It is very simple. All you do is stand up, put one hand towards the ceiling, and jump up five times and exclaim, "I am happy!" Do it again one, two, three... Do it with both hands in the air if you really want to feel great!

Yes! I love zest!

This was taught to me by one of my mentors' named Jinendra Swami whose job title is Messenger of Sustainable Happiness. He focuses on the physiological experience of happiness. This exercise allows us to feel happy without having to *think* ourselves into getting there.

I have a number of clients who instead of eating a candy bar at the mid-afternoon work lull, go to the bathroom, enter the stall for privacy, and do their five "I am happy!" jumps!

You will feel a rush of exhilaration and zestful happiness inside.

In fact, if you are unable to exclaim, "I am happy!" you can simply mouth the words and still get the same effect.

In the morning routine, I recommend doing this after your laughter practice.

GRATITUDE PRACTICE

Creating a gratitude practice in your life is important.

I recommend doing this as part of your morning routine. You can start the gratitude practice after your five "I am happy!" jumps.

The gratitude practice is crucial. Gratitude is another character strength that stimulates happiness. The more you develop your gratitude the happier you are going to be.

How will you adopt a gratitude practice in your daily routine?

There are different opportunities for you to input a gratitude practice in your life such as while showering, driving, walking, jogging, singing, drinking coffee, or journaling.

First, identify how you are going to adopt a gratitude practice into your day to day routine. What is the thing you already do every day that will be easy to incorporate into this practice?

Secondly, set the parameters for length of time.

Once you determine the activity you will be doing for your gratitude practice, then set the parameters. For example, if you are going to do a gratitude shower, decide the entire time you wash your body you will be in gratitude. Alternatively, you could be in gratitude for the duration of one song or while you are driving, walking, or jogging from point A to point B. If you choose to do a journal, decide to write ten things for which you are grateful.

Third, never repeat so you can expand your gratitude awareness.

The next point of the gratitude practice is to never, ever repeat. This is very important because you want to consistently expand your gratitude awareness. You are smart, and you will get bored if you say the same things over and over. Therefore, I recommend using different subjects or topics per day. For instance, one day you focus on your family, another day you focus on your city, another day you focus on your job, or your home, or the food in your refrigerator, or your body. You can be grateful for anything you can think!

My mentor, Jinendra Swami, told me, "Aymee, if you are breathing you need to be grateful," and it is true.

We are alive, we are experiencing life, and

this is absolutely something to cherish.

Fourth, I propose using the statement: "I am grateful for _____ because it adds _____ to my life."

This brings me to the next point of the gratitude practice - you need to focus on the heart based wisdom of the thing for which you express gratitude. For instance, instead of "I am grateful for my dog" you want to focus on the unconditional love and companionship that your dog adds to your life.

Adopt this method of creating a gratitude practice as a daily experience, and you will definitely boost your mood. You can be happier any time you want.

MORNING ROUTINE TIMING

Everyone gets up in the morning and has certain things to do every day. This morning routine will work into anyone's existing daily routine.

Go through each activity to see how long you think each one will take....

Wake up and smile = 2 seconds

"Today is the happiest day of my life!" = 3 seconds

5 Duchenne smile push ups = 1 minute

Laughter practice = 5 seconds

5 "I am happy!" jumps = 10 seconds

Gratitude Practice = 1 minute

Total Time = 2 minutes and 20 seconds

Seriously?! In two minutes and twenty seconds you will be able to create a sustained, positive mood for a few hours! Incredible!

Do you have two minutes within your morning routine to perform happiness activities? Smiling? Setting a positive intention? Laughing? Reminiscing about happy memories? Laugh a little? Jump for joy? Express Gratitude?

Sounds pretty easy! And worthwhile! Give it a whirl, and let me know how it goes!

I created a protocol sheet that is available for you in Appendix A so you can track your progress.

In my experience, this two minute and twenty second routine will give you a positive mood for up to approximately five hours.

When you notice the decline in your mood, the morning routine is wearing off. Then you are ready to begin the daytime routine.

DAYTIME ROUTINE

When you notice your positive mood is wearing off, start the daytime routine. This routine incorporates acts of kindness, exercise, positive language, positive thinking, and living in the moment.

Adopting these practices is absolutely the most exciting thing you could be doing for yourself because happiness is the goal of all goals.

Working on your happiness is you perfecting the bullseye of life.

In fact, think about it. You do _____ to be happy, and you do _____ to be happy, and you do _____ to be happy. Instead of getting happiness as a byproduct, you are going to

focus on creating happiness

within yourself right now.

In the daytime routine there are two sink or swim concepts: Positive Thinking and Living in the Moment. As you will be adopting all the activities in the daily routine, the ones you absolutely must master are positive thinking and living in the moment.

KINDNESS PRACTICE

When you finish the morning routine, you will notice you have a high positive mood for a few hours. When you feel a dip in your mood start your five acts of kindness. Science has shown if you do five acts of kindness a day, you will become happier. I understand this seems simple. Remember that happiness is different from rocket science. It is a matter of that on which you focus.

These acts of kindness can be any type, small or large. It is so easy to do acts of kindness these days. You can simply post a nice message on someone's social media, send someone a sweet text message, compliment someone on their smile, or say, "Hey, that color looks good on you." Even simply petting a dog on the street or picking up trash from the ground count as acts of kindness.

Perform five acts of kindness a day.

I recommend setting an alarm around 11am or 12pm to go off daily to remind you to do your acts of kindness right there and then.

Visit the Acts of Kindness Foundation website to find out more information and receive daily emails with ideas for various acts of kindness.

You are probably a kind person. There is a part of you that is already kind, and you are probably doing kind things already every day. This is an opportunity for you to feel kind within the act. Instead of obligatory kindness by rote such as opening the door for the person holding grocery bags, you are going to allow genuine kindness to flood your body. Savor the kindness inside you as you are opening the door. Really get into feeling kind in that moment when you are performing the act of kindness.

Five acts of kindness will increase your mood.

If you wanted to do more, you could. I know there are overachievers out there so if you want to apply your overachieving personality to happiness, it definitely would pay off, and I highly encourage it!

It gives me a happiness boost thinking about the effort you are going to put into creating your happiness practice every day.

POSITIVE LANGUAGE

Positive language is absolutely crucial to incorporate throughout your daily experience.

This means eliminate: "no", "not", "don't", "can't", "should", "but", and "try".

Instead of "no" you are going to say "I would prefer" or "I would rather."

Instead of "not" or any conjunction of "not" you are going to say what you can do. For example, "Don't go on the grass" versus, "Stay on the sidewalk."

This emphasizes how you want your upward spiral to go by identifying what you can do.

Instead of "should" you are going to eliminate it and say "I recommend" if it is geared toward someone else or "I am doing it" if it is for yourself.

Instead of "but" you are going to say "yet" or "and".

And simply eliminate "try". One of my mentors said, "Aymee, 'try' is an admittance of failure, and I know you are going to be happier."

You are NOT going to TRY to be happier.

This conscious emphasis of creating an upward spiral using positive language is going to really help you. This is because you are going to notice an absence of negative language. Negative language indicates negative thoughts, and if you have made The Happiness Decision, you are eliminating all negative thoughts.

Put a sticky note on your computer or your phone that says:

"Eliminate: no, not, don't, can't, should, but, try."

If you bring awareness to your electronic communication by eliminating these words, you will see a difference in how you feel and how others feel around you when you are communicating. Converting to positive language is very, very important. It requires a lot of diligence, discipline, and perseverance; it pays off.

While you become aware of how you use these words, counteract the sentence right away with:

"What I meant to say was..."

Your happiness will absolutely increase, and you will definitely feel better if you simply eliminate "no", "not", "don't", "can't", "should", "but", and "try" to create a positive language practice in your day to day experience.

This is one of the more challenging practices in the Happiness Makeover®. You have been saying negative language for years! Imagine if I could make everyone a positive speaker with a snap of a finger. Impossible right?! This is why happiness is work. Here is an example of negative and positive language:

Negative Language

There is no way I am going to be able to stop using negative words. I don't know how I would ever do it. I probably can't do it even if I tried. So

I won't do it. Even though I should do it. It probably isn't that bad for me if I try it. I may try it.

Positive Language

I really want to do my best in this Happiness Makeover™. I am going to give it my all and use positive language as much as possible. It may be challenging, yet I know I can do it. I need to do this! I will do it!

Which one leads to positivity? Which one sounds happier? Which one would make you happier?

Let's do an exercise. I am going to ask you a series of obvious "no" questions, and you respond with "I would rather" or "I would prefer":

Do you want to give all your money to the government?

Do you want to wear the same pair of jeans every day?

Do you want to stay in college forever?

OK, do you get the picture? You want to reinforce what you *do* want in life instead of spending any time at all talking about what is undesirable.

Persistence pays off with the positive language practice.

POSITIVE THINKING

Positive thinking is absolutely crucial to your happiness practice because

when you are thinking negatively, you are unhappy.

There has to be effort towards becoming a positive thinker and eliminating all negative thoughts.

Identify your average positive to negative thought ratio. If you are mostly negative, you have a lot of work ahead of you.

The goal is to convert entirely into a positive thinker, and you can do it if you follow the guidelines I have outlined here.

This is a crucial

sink or swim component

of the daytime routine.

If you fail within this aspect of the program, you will be unhappy. You have to concentrate extra hard on this specific lesson. Becoming a positive thinker must be one of the most important priorities in your happiness practice.

Here are my recommendations of how to become a positive thinker. First, purchase an 'Inner Colleague Creation Book'. Go to a drug store and purchase a small memo pad with a binding on the side. This is likely to be relatively inexpensive yet *very* worthwhile. Throughout the day when you experience a negative thought, you write it on the left side of the page; convert it to a positive on the right side of the page (write the opposite of the negative thought on the right hand side of the page). Any negative thought I consider Inner Critic, and any positive thought I consider Inner Colleague.

Instead of going into rumination of negative thought after negative thought you can stop the rumination right away by getting out your Inner Colleague Creation Book and convert the Inner Critic thought to an Inner Colleague thought in the moment it occurs.

One important point:

You have to do it in the moment.

The moment the negative thought occurs, excuse yourself from whatever you are doing, and go to your Inner Colleague Creation Book. Write down the negative thought, and convert it to a positive thought as soon as possible. If you wait, you are only hurting your happiness. It is very important that you convert a negative thought the moment it occurs into a positive in your Inner Colleague Creation Book throughout the entire day.

I AM UNABLE TO EMPHASIZE THIS ENOUGH!

IF YOU FOREGO THIS PRACTICE,

YOU WILL BE UNHAPPIER.

I had clients say, I am going to sit here and convert my Inner Critic to my Inner Colleague all day long.

You know what I say to them?

"Well, that would be the best possible use of your time."

Your negative thoughts constrict your brain, and positive thoughts expand your brain. Ultimately, we want to live our best life with our brains expanded instead of constricted.

This is why you want to put effort into creating a positive thinking practice within your daily happiness practice.

It is absolutely crucial.

As you spend time converting your negative thoughts to positive thoughts, you will begin to see a negative thought pattern emerge.

Notice your negative thought patterns. Are you having negative thoughts about yourself? Others? Circumstances?

This exercise is definitely about thoughts instead of beliefs. Beliefs are different from thoughts. For example, if your negative thought is "I hate my boss", you would convert it to "I love my boss" because you are following my guidance in this exercise. Of course you are unable to *believe* that you 'love your boss' if you really hate your boss because you wrote it down in your notebook. What you are doing is stopping rumination and creating a vision of what to work towards so you can proceed with the positive. We address your belief system through another exercise called "Weeding Out Your Garden of Happiness".

Your belief system most likely was developed from your interpretation of experiences from the ages of zero to six. This interpretation formed your subconscious which is operating your daily experiences by influencing your beliefs, which influence your thoughts, which influence your emotions, which influence your behavior.

Belief - Thought - Emotion - Behavior

Identifying your negative thought pattern allows you to go deeper into your psychology so you can access your underlying subconscious beliefs which are triggering your negative thoughts.

You must challenge your belief system

to see if it is in fact even true!

Most belief systems I have found are false!

Keep reading about how to "Weed Out Your Garden of Happiness" of these negative beliefs to do the deeper psychological work.

GARDEN OF HAPPINESS

This is another crucial element to sustaining your happiness. My clients make The Happiness Decision, and they forsake all negative thoughts.

I know negative thoughts will continue despite making The Happiness Decision. It is important to identify your own negative thinking patterns. What types of negative thoughts are you having? Are they about yourself? Are they about your family? Are they about your job? What are they about? Through gaining awareness of your negative thinking patterns you can identify and challenge the underlying subconscious beliefs. I consider the negative subconscious belief to be the root of a weed in your garden of happiness.

Belief - Thought - Emotion - Behavior

You may realize you feel unhappy when you are feeling unhappy. However, this is really the tip of the iceberg. Before you have a feeling, you have a thought that is triggered by a subconscious belief.

It takes a lot of awareness to be able to find the one particular negative thought that is triggering the emotion and, therefore, influencing the behavior.

For example, a negative thought is "I can't do it." That could lead to the emotion of unhappiness and the behaviors of lethargy and isolation.

I can't do it [thought] - unhappiness [emotion]

- lethargy & isolation [behavior]

This exercise of weeding your garden of happiness is a method to determine the root belief system in your subconscious. Ready? Make sure you are alone and will be undisturbed.

You can access your subconscious through this particular exercise:

1. *Identify a negative thought or a recurring negative thought.*

2. *Sit with this negative thought for a moment.*

3. *Go into your heart space to identify the underlying belief of this thought:*

Take a deep breath. Eyes are closed.

Put one hand on your heart, one hand on your belly.

Take another deep breath.

Drop your attention into your heart center.

Focus your awareness into the area of your heart.

Focus on creating an all loving, all nurturing, all accepting, open environment there.

Allow your heartbeat to come through your chest to the palm of your hand.

When you feel your heartbeat ask yourself, "What is the underlying belief?"

Wait for an inner response.

Ask the next question, "Is this the root belief?"

Wait for the response.

When you hear the answer, challenge it.

"Is _____ the root belief?" and wait for a response.

If the answer is "No," you have to dig deeper and ask again.

Then wait.

When your heart answers again, challenge it.

"Is _____ the root belief?"

Repeat until your heart is complete.

When your heart is affirmative and you feel confident you have identified the root belief in your subconscious, you have determined the root of the weed in your garden of happiness.

IDENTIFY YOUR WEED

I'm not good enough - I can't do it - unhappy - lethargy & isolation

    [belief]   **[thought]**   **[emotion]**   **[behavior]**

When you clearly understand the root belief of this particular thought, take a deep breath and open your eyes.

You are coming back to your conscious self from your subconscious.

4. Ask yourself: Is this true?

For example, I have witnessed many overachieving, amazing people who hold the belief:

"I'm not good enough."

Obviously, we can rationalize this as FALSE!

Is it true that you have been holding a false belief which is triggering you to negative thinking, which is triggering negative emotional experiences, and, therefore, guiding you into negative behavioral patterns?

Is this a truly accurate experience in your life?

Have you really believed that?

Have you really been thinking that, feeling like that, and behaving like that?

Most likely the answers are "YES".

Challenge this belief.

Let's use "I'm not good enough" as an example.

Is this belief really true?

Have you been able to handle life? Have you been able to accomplish your goals? Have you been able to go to college? Have you been on a winning team? Is this belief really true?

Most likely it is false.

Most likely something happened to you between the age of zero to six where you were made to believe this as the truth. Do you really believe this now? We can have non-attachment around this belief. All we need to do is recognize that something might have happened to you (a sibling was born, you were hungry, a toy was taken away or worse) during your first six years of life that made you believe this.

Are you old enough to choose your own belief system now?

YES!

Do you want a belief system which operates on the truth?

YES!

Do you want a belief system that guides your upward spiral?

You are old enough to choose your belief system so you want to choose a belief system that is going to support your upward spiral instead of inhibit your upward spiral or even worse, create a downward spiral.

You need to eradicate the root belief within this weed in your garden of happiness and now...

5. *Plant a flower in alignment with the truth. For example,*

"I am amazing!"

This is the truth!

You are amazing. Do you really believe that? Do you want to believe that? Are you ready to update your consciousness to the truth? This is a moment of awakening where you decide to update your VHS psychology to MP3 psychology.

Is this new belief in your upward spiral?

If you were truly *believing* "I am amazing!", what would you be *thinking*? "I can do anything!" If you were thinking "I can do anything!", how would you *feel*? You would feel happy. Through this feeling of happiness, your behavior would be to make your dreams come true.

PLANT A FLOWER

**I am amazing - I can do anything   - happy -   motivation &
                                                   inspiration**

[belief]   [thought]   [emotion]   [behavior]

In order for you to effectively weed out your garden of happiness of
negative beliefs, you *must*

fertilize the new flower 5,000 times.

However many times you have had the identified negative thought, you
must counter it 5,000 times in order to make significant change. Think
about how many cells are in your body or stars in the sky to put that
number into perspective. When considering significant psychological
change, it requires work and effort to change. This is the most rewarding
work you could ever do!

YOU MUST WEED YOUR GARDEN OF HAPPINESS OF NEGATIVE BELIEFS!

Weed out your garden of happiness of these negative beliefs for EVERY
SINGLE one of your recurring negative thoughts.

Ultimately, you want to have zero negative beliefs, triggering zero
negative thoughts, zero negative emotions, and zero negative behaviors.
This will put you in alignment with your intention of forsaking all
negative thoughts as indicated in your signed Happiness Decision.

Becoming a positive thinker takes time, effort, diligence, and
perseverance. You can do it if you commit to doing the work.

Work on your garden of happiness

by weeding and planting flowers.

LIVING IN THE MOMENT

Harvard research has shown that 47% of the time people are thinking about something other than what they are actually doing in the moment.

I have approximately a 50% chance you are truly listening to what I have to say.

I do recommend putting a lot of effort into this.

Take good notes and revisit this chapter as frequently as possible until you arrive in the now.

The journey into the now could be one that takes a lot of effort and time.

In fact, it took me six months of active training to arrive in the now.

However, when I did arrive in the now, a huge amount of stress was relieved from my shoulders.

I thought I had my happiness perfected, however, once I fine-tuned my awareness to be *in this moment* it took my happiness to a whole new level.

I created these steps through my own experience of learning how to live in this moment:

1. *Be aware you are out of the moment. Realize your thoughts are in the past or the future.*

2. *You get three options: (a) fishing rod (b) raft (c) fireplace.*

    a)   Close your eyes, and visualize yourself with a fishing rod. The fishing line is already cast far away. That fishing line is a symbol of your thoughts that are in the past or in the future. Reel in the fishing line back to the here and now, and when you can see the end of the fishing line go to step three.

b) Close your eyes, and visualize yourself on a lovely day on a beautiful lake. You are in the lake next to a raft. Go ahead and see yourself getting onto the raft, laying down, and feeling the sun's warmth on your body. Then go to step three.

c) Close your eyes, and visualize yourself sitting next to a fireplace feeling the fire's warmth on your body. When you can feel the fire's warmth on your body, go to step three.

Make a mental note to yourself - are you option (a), (b), or (c)? Use the visual that is the easiest for you or whichever one makes you happiest. Go through the visualization, and then open your eyes.

3. *What is going on with your senses?*

Check in with your senses - touch, taste, sound, sight, and hearing. Say, "I'm seeing _____, I'm hearing _____, I'm tasting _____, I'm smelling _____, I'm touching_____."

This has to be a physical experience. Make it easy, simple, and one sentence per sense.

NOTE Stay away from the word "feel" because that word connotes an emotional experience, and we are going for a physical experience.

4. *Ask your heart, "What is the gift in this moment?"*

Go into your heart space.

Close your eyes and take a deep breath. Place both feet on the ground.

Put one hand on your heart, one hand on your belly.

Drop your awareness into your heart center.

Take a deep breath.

One more time for good measure.

Drop your awareness into your heart center.

Focus your attention in the area of your heart.

Focus on creating an all loving, all nurturing, all accepting,

open environment there.

You can also imagine the last time you went to the airport to pick up someone you love.

Cultivate this feeling in your heart center.

When you feel like it has been achieved, allow your heartbeat

to come through your chest to the palm of your hand.

When you feel your heartbeat, ask yourself, to your heart,

"What is the gift in this moment?"

Wait for a response.

Ask, "Anything else?"

Wait for a response.

Repeat until your heart is complete.

There may be multiple gifts in this moment, and you want to ensure you are gleaning all the gifts you are meant to receive right now.

5. *Gratitude for the gifts in step four.*

Use the structure, "I am grateful for _____ gift (fill in the blank with each of the gifts from step four) because it adds _____ to my life."

This deepens your sense of gratitude in your heart.

If you suffer from anxiety or ADHD, you can help yourself by following these five steps to living in the moment. Bringing all your awareness into this moment, receiving the gifts in this moment, and having gratitude for those gifts will help you focus and be more productive. It is going to help you get to places on time and offer you greater peace and contentment.

All of the benefits you receive once you have done the work of arriving in the now are truly remarkable.

You have to do this at least 50% of your day because the Harvard study showed 47% of the time you are probably thinking of something other than what you are doing in the moment.

Go through these 5 daytime steps 100 times a day.

That is once every five minutes for an eight-hour time period. I understand it may sound like a lot, however, it is about doing the work to arrive in the now. Once you have done these steps so many times you will be permanently in the now, never wanting to leave because it is so amazing in this moment!

I have been living in the moment since 2004, and I have trained many others to live in the now! It is possible!

I understand you can only live in the moment to a certain extent, and there is a need to plan sometimes as well as occasionally savor the past. However, mostly we want to be here now.

Schedule a time to plan.

For example, let's say you are thinking about a dinner arrangement you have at seven, and it is three in the afternoon.

You might be thinking, "Where am I going to go? What am I going to wear? How am I going to get there? Who is going to be there? Am I going to like the food?"

Whatever it is, instead of thinking about it all day long, you are going to *schedule a time to think about it*, so let's say six o'clock you have to make all of the decisions that relate to the dinner at seven. This frees you to live in the moment between three and six.

In addition to learning the five steps, scheduling a time to plan, savoring positive memories of the past, you have to...

Fasten Your Happiness Seat Belt!

Here are two quick steps you can use to boost your mood by living in the moment.

The seat belt in your car has two straps: one goes over your shoulder and one goes over your waist.

The Happiness Seat Belt also has *two straps*: the strap over your shoulder is *live in this moment*, and the one over your waist is *choose happiness*.

Without your Happiness Seat Belt,

it is a wild ride!

Let's practice it right now.

We will start with the steps to living in the moment you learned earlier. For The Happiness Seat Belt, let's begin with step two instead of step one in these steps to living in the moment because we will assume you are out of this moment now (step one of living in the moment is being aware you are out of this moment, thinking of something in the past or the future). Therefore, we will begin with step two:

Step 2: Pick the visualization below that makes you the happiest and is the easiest.

Close your eyes. Visualize yourself with a fishing line that is cast far away. You are going to reel the line back to the here and now. It is a symbol of your thoughts in the past or future. When you can see the end of the fishing line open your eyes and go to step three.

Visualize yourself in a lake next to a raft. See yourself get on top of the raft, and feel the sun's warmth on your body. When you can see yourself on top of that raft open your eyes and go to step three.

Visualize yourself sitting next to a fireplace, and feel the fire's warmth on your body. When you feel the fire's warmth on your body open your eyes and go to step three.

Step 3: Check in with your senses.

I'm seeing _____, I'm hearing _____, I'm tasting _____, I'm smelling _____, I'm touching _____.

OK, and now we are going to go to step four.

Step 4: Ask your heart, "What is the gift in this moment?"

Place both feet on the ground. Close your eyes.

Put one hand on your heart and one hand on your belly.

Take a deep breath.

Drop your awareness into your heart center, and

focus your attention in the area of your heart.

Focus on creating an all loving, all nurturing, all accepting,

open environment there.

Allow your heartbeat to come through your chest to the palm of your hand.

When you can feel your heartbeat, ask your heart, "What is the gift in this moment?"

Wait for a response.

When the gift comes to you, ask, "Anything else?"

Wait for a response.

Repeat, "Anything else?"

Wait for the response.

Continue to ask, "Anything else?" until your heart is complete.

Step 5: Gratitude for the gifts in this moment.

Repeat, "I am grateful for _____ (fill in the blank with the gifts in this moment from step four), because it adds _____ to my life."

There you have it.

You have achieved a different state of consciousness.

This is a new state of awareness after following

the five steps to living in the moment.

THE VORTEX!

You may have arrived in the now for the very first time.

Are you experiencing calm, centeredness, certainty, or a difference in any way? A presence? Present in the moment?

Welcome to the now! The trick is to stay here, and this is where the hundred times a day comes in.

I have clients who set mindfulness bells on their cell phones or get vibrating time watches so they can follow through with the direction of a hundred times a day. I encourage you to use tools to support you in this change.

The students who use support tools get the best results.

I have noticed throughout my practice people feel a sense of calm and peace as well as an absence of frustration, disappointment, stress, and fear when they have arrived in this moment.

Working on bringing yourself into the now is extremely beneficial for you.

IF YOU SKIP PRACTICING

THESE FIVE STEPS TO LIVING IN THE MOMENT

AT LEAST 100 TIMES A DAY

WITH GREAT EFFORT,

YOUR SUSTAINABLE HAPPINESS

WILL SUFFER.

EXERCISE

Exercise has been proven to be more effective than antidepressants.

Our bodies are made to move, and you may be stuck in a sedentary lifestyle.

This may look like sitting in a car on the way to work, sitting at work for eight hours, sitting in the car on the way back home, sitting on the couch to watch television, and then laying in bed.

Unless we consciously build exercise into our daily schedules, it is challenging to fit it in our busy yet laissez faire lifestyles.

Every day I hear excuses about how you are without enough time in the day to exercise. This seems wild to me! At just about any time, you can run in place, do a hundred jumping jacks, or do fifty squats. Between sitting at the computer or in front of the television, or even in your cubicle at work, I am confident you can make time to 'work your body'.

Exercise at least twenty minutes every day which includes walking.

If you can exercise outside, great! If you can make it a social event, great!

Commit to exercise, and make it a priority.

I learned the value of exercise the hard way. I had to lose thirty pounds three times in my life due to inactivity and poor eating habits. Now I exercise regularly, eat healthier, and cleanse regularly which helps me feel good and healthy.

In the Happiness Makeover® program, I recommend yoga or the P90X home exercise for a 90-day exercise program.

In summary, if you commit to a daily practice of kindness, present moment living, positive thinking, positive speaking, and exercise, you will achieve a frequent positive mood throughout the day.

TIMING OF THE DAYTIME ROUTINE

Since the daytime routine focuses on positive thinking, acts of kindness, living in the moment, positive speech, and walking at the very minimum, the time commitment is minimal yet intensive. Other than walking, exercising, or performing an act of kindness here or there, you are quite simply mindful of your thoughts, your words, and gleaning the best from every single moment.

This program is an immersion. It is jumping into your happy life with both feet from the beginning and learning how to do it as you go along - one step at a time, one moment at a time. Yet when practiced consistently day in and day out phenomenal results occur.

You will see magic and rainbows with your own eyes!

So far the morning routine is two minutes and twenty seconds, and the daytime routine is all day long in the form of awareness of yourself through your thoughts, words, and actions.

SLEEP ROUTINE

Self awareness only grows in reflection. It is important to end each day in a way that aids our upward spiral.

Ending the day on a good note is the goal of the sleep routine which is

easy as 1-2-3!

1. *Recount your five acts of kindness from the daytime routine.*

    You can do this at the dinner table in discussion with your family, or you can do this by yourself. You can even do this by writing down your acts of kindness. It is up to you. Explore all options.

2. *Ask yourself, "What are three good things that happened today? How did I contribute to them?"*

    Add this to the dinner discussion among your family or friends. Or you could say it to yourself or write it down. Do whatever makes you happiest.

3. *Read to yourself the positive thoughts of the day from your Inner Colleague Creation Book.*

Step 3 is going to shift your subconscious.

Often our negative thought patterns are created between the ages of zero and six and are consistently hammering us throughout the day. We want to reinforce the changes in your subconsciousness that you did during your weeding out of your garden of happiness exercise. The best way to do this is right before you go to sleep.

This will gradually help you become a positive thinker over time.

If you are really wanting significant change and you suffer from physical ailments, I recommend making a positive thought prescription created from the thoughts introduced by Louise Hay in her book "You Can Heal Your Life". Go through her list and identify all of the ailments you have ever had in your entire life. After reading the positive thoughts of the day from your Inner Colleague Creation Book, read to yourself your personalized "Positive Thought Prescription".

As a bonus, if you are attuned to Reiki energy, give yourself a healing right after you complete the reading of the Inner Colleague Creation Book and your Positive Thought Prescription.

This will help create a more positive subconscious over time.

TIMING OF THE SLEEP ROUTINE

The sleep routine offers a nice way to end the day with yourself or with your loved ones. How long does each activity take?

Recount your acts of kindness = 30 seconds

What are three good things, and how did I contribute? = 1 minute

Inner Colleague Creation Thoughts of the Day = 2 minutes

(Recommended for those with physical pain) Positive Thought Prescription = 2 minutes

(Optional for those attuned in Reiki) Reiki for 10 minutes

TOTAL = 5 minutes 30 seconds

Do you have five minutes and thirty seconds for your happiness every night?

I sure hope so!

All in all, you have the morning routine (two minutes and twenty seconds), the daytime routine (all day long), and the sleep routine (five minutes and thirty seconds). This equals:

TOTAL = 7 minutes and 60 seconds

ALL HAPPINESS ROUTINES TOTAL TIME

+ DAILY CONSCIOUS AWARENESS

Do you have less than 8 minutes a day to devote to a

happiness practice in your day to day life?

The answer better be "YES"!

NOTE: See Appendix A for a Happiness Makeover® Protocol Chart to aid in accountability for adopting the new practice of happiness science.

STEP 2 MASTERY

When you notice your mood is generally positive and you have the ability to give yourself a positive mood any time you want, regardless of where you are, who you are with, or what you are doing, then you have mastered step two.

Put yourself on a Weekly Grading System.

After practicing the routines for a few days, give yourself a grade: A, B, C, D, or E. Give yourself a grade on each routine once a week and notice where you are performing well as well as where you need improvement:

Morning Routine -

Daytime Routine -

Sleep Routine -

Positive to Negative Thought Ratio -

In the Moment % -

If you notice your numbers are down, your mood will suffer. If your numbers are up, your mood will be positive. Constantly check in with how you are doing with building this happiness practice into your daily life. We can always do better!

Lead with the activities you most enjoy, and

build in the others as you start getting the hang of it.

You have to work up to being an Olympian in happiness. Give yourself time and space for a realistic learning curve. Before we learn calculus, we first need arithmetic and algebra. It is the same thing in happiness. You will notice a consistent improvement in your skill development as well as your positive mood.

CHAPTER 4: RESILIENCY

STEP 3 – OVERCOME HAPPINESS CHALLENGES

Resiliency is a crux for sustainable happiness. It will make you or break you. Everyone has challenges in life. In sustainable happiness, your only option is to persevere like a Happiness Olympian and use the tools I will introduce. Let's say you have been doing a great job at taking charge of your own happiness, and you have been feeling great since adopting the new routine system. You have been empowered over your own happiness for maybe the first time in your life. You have been doing the routines consistently and feeling so positive and...

BAM!

You get a left hook from life!

You get fired. Your spouse asks for a divorce. You get in a car accident. You have to go bankrupt. You have a bad hair day.

Fill in the blank with any negative circumstance you may encounter any time, any day. This happens to everyone! The trick to sustainable happiness is different from ignoring the 'bad' things that happen every day; it is to handle them in the best possible way.

I am going to equip you with the best tools happiness science has to offer besides the mood boosting techniques in the daily routines.

These tools are to be used when your happiness is being challenged beyond what any happiness booster can do for you.

In the moment when you realize something is happening where you are losing your happiness, use these tools to combat the challenge so you can come out on top - laughing at your happiness challenges!

Using these tools will aid you in developing resiliency to learn lessons of life and handle all circumstances like a cool, calm, and collected firefighter in the midst of the burning building.

I recommend practicing the happiness challenge tools in everyday life first so when you have a challenge you will be well practiced.

HAPPINESS SHIELD

This is one of the most important tools of the entire Happiness Makeover®.

It is made from the five top strengths of the Values in Action (VIA) Character Strengths. The VIA Character Strengths are the positive psychology opposite of the traditional psychology Disorder Manual (DSM). Instead of psychology telling you what is wrong with you, I can focus on what is *right* about you.

Out of the 24 strengths, there are five top strengths which need to be developed for you to feel happier. Those strengths are kindness, love, optimism, gratitude, and zest (KLOGZ). When it comes to fighting off happiness challenges, if you use your KLOGZ, you will end up laughing at the challenge! I am serious.

Read these instructions then draw away! Grab a pencil and paper, and draw a large box. Then draw a stick figure with a smiley face, and put some hair on it. That is you.

Now draw a horizontal line underneath the stick figure like it is the ground, and then put a circle around the entire body of the stick figure.

Write the word "happy" all over the white space between the stick figure and the circle, "happy" under the legs, on top of the head, over and over.

This is you making The Happiness Decision.

Write these words on the outside of the circle (so the words become the circle): kindness, love, optimism, gratitude, and zest.

Kindness, Love, Optimism, Gratitude, and Zest

Draw four asterisks or stars on the outside of the circle.

Label them as person, place, thing, and circumstance.

Underneath the diagram write the question,

"How can I use _____ to protect my happiness?"

In the blank, write "KLOGZ" (kindness, love, optimism, gratitude, and zest).

The Happiness Shield is

your KLOGZ between

your happiness

and

every person, place, thing, or circumstance.

In learning sustainable happiness, you have to learn how to sustain your happiness in the face of adversity.

Hold your happiness challenge tools in the forefront of your mind ready for the next person, place, thing, or circumstance that aims to create unhappiness for you.

The question is:

"HOW do I use KLOGZ to protect my happiness?"

You have to use all five at the same time. It is unable to work if you use only one, two, or three of the strengths. You need all five.

Here is an example of how to use KLOGZ.

Who has an unhappy family member? Whether it is mom, sister, brother, dad, whoever it is, you are going to respond with KLOGZ. Let's say your mom is having a bad day, and you really want to respond with your KLOGZ.

Mom is complaining about her bad day, and you have a couple of choices.

You can say, "Mom that really sucks," and agree with her.

You can respond with more complaining. Misery does love company.

However, instead you can intercept with KLOGZ!

Kindness - I admire _____

Love - I accept _____

Optimism - I am optimistic _____

Gratitude - I am grateful _____

Zest - I am excited _____

Now practice.

Mom says, "Grumble, grumble, grumble."

You respond with your KLOGZ!

"Mom, I *admire* how you always tell me how you really feel.

I *accept* you are having a bad day today.

I am *optimistic* things will improve.

I am *grateful* for this time we do have to spend together.

I am *excited* for lunch!"

In regards to kindness, you can always think of it as admiration. When people get admired something softens them inside. When was the last time you were admired by your loved ones? Everyone can use more admiration in their lives.

Start your KLOGZ with kindness:

"Mom, I admire how you always tell me how you really feel."

Love is unconditional acceptance:

"I accept that you are having a bad day today."

Use realistic optimism:

"I am optimistic things will improve because I just arrived, and

we are about to go have a great lunch."

Sometimes optimism gets a bad rap. It is important you maintain realistic optimism. It is best to understand realistic optimism through an example:

A Pessimist stands at the bottom of a mountain, looks at the top, and says,

"There is no way that I am going to get to the top."

An Optimist stands at the bottom of the mountain and says,

"I can see myself at the top and am going to go for the gold. Here I go!"

A Realistic Optimist stands at the bottom of the mountain and says,

"I will prepare myself for the journey. I am going to bring two pairs of shoes, enough water, another sweater, and I can see myself at the top."

Right now, I have a smile on my face.

Realistic optimism is having an *achievable goal* with a *realistic plan* and *believing in yourself* to achieve the plan.

Next is gratitude followed by zest.

Gratitude is having a sense of thanks for something in your life.

Zest is enthusiasm and excitement in life. You are *sizzling the bacon*! It is so important you add a few exclamations into your life. It is OK to pump it up with some enthusiasm.

Kindness, Love, Optimism, Gratitude, and Zest

Back to the conversation with Mom...

Mom says, "Grumble, grumble, grumble."

You say,

"Mom, I *admire* how you can share your feelings openly with me.

I *accept* you are having a bad day today.

I am *optimistic* things will improve

since I just arrived, and we are about to go to lunch.

I am *grateful* we have this time to spend together.

I am *excited* to go to lunch!"

Do you feel happier just by reading that? Did you get a happiness boost? This is happiness science at its best!

For the Happiness Overachievers, if you want to add a bonus to the Happiness Shield, use *affection*.

"Mom, come here, I want to give you a *hug!*"

I have a big smile on my face right after using KLOGZ.

That is the beauty of happiness science and emotional contagion.

In 2008 there was a Harvard study that showed happiness spread up to three degrees of separation of every single person to whom you came into contact. You are influencing up to three degrees of separation in your daily life.

Write down the number of people you talk to, look at, email, and interact on social media with in a day. Exponentially multiply that times three, and that is how much your happiness is worth to me!

That is How Much your Happiness is Worth to the World.

I know you want to see a positive change in this world.

Your happiness decision is your first priority because we can only be the change we want to see. You want to see happier people in this world, I am sure. This starts with you and your decision to be responsible for your own happiness.

Use your Happiness Shield, KLO6Z,

to ward off unhappiness

and turn any challenge into laughter.

POLLYANNA'S GAME

I learned about Pollyanna's game from my mentor, Dr. Bob Nozik, who has been sustainably happy since 1987. His book "Happy 4 Life: Here's How to Do It" is the only required reading in the Happiness Makeover™ program. He has an entire chapter on Pollyanna's game and how to use it. When Dr. Bob gives short speeches he always talks about his quickest way to happiness which is Pollyanna's Game.

Pollyanna is a character in a book that was written in 1912. She was the daughter of a minister of a poor congregation and raised by him as her mother passed while giving birth. She was dependent on handouts from the church for everything. Once Pollyanna heard there was going to be a doll for a little girl in the handouts, and she was very excited. When the handouts came there were zero dolls. In fact there was nothing for a little girl at all; there were only crutches for a child. She was very upset. Her Dad never liked seeing Pollyanna upset so he asked her, "Pollyanna, what can you be glad about with these crutches?" She thought about it for days. Stumped without an answer, she came back to her father for advisement. He said, "Pollyanna, you are you without needing the crutches." This started their "Just be Glad" game.

Dr. Bob uses the terminology "Pollyanna's Game" as a way of seeing the good in the bad.

Remember happiness is different from rocket science. I have a surprise for you:

Every "bad thing" that happened in your past

led to something good.

If you went through and broke down every single bad thing that happened to you, more than likely you can find something good that came out of it.

Have you ever looked to your body, beauty, bank account, marriage, or health for your happiness? Most likely your happiness suffers if all or any of those were failing you.

However, I have been able to maintain my happiness even when I was faced with intense adversities. The incredible lesson born from these challenges was:

My happiness is on the inside regardless

of what is happening on the outside.

For me this was HUGE.

For an exercise, think about all of the bad things that ever happened to you. Then think about all the good things that came from them. Prove it to yourself. As soon as something bad happens use Pollyanna's Game to see the silver lining.

One of my mentors, Louise Hay encourages people encountering a problem to focus on the belief "Out of the situation only good will come." It is your perceived idea that this is a 'problem'. However, some sort of blessing is going to come out of it. Focus on something good that is going to come out of the situation immediately, and you will be surprised how quickly the gift comes.

For example, you get a flat tire on the way to an important meeting and have to miss it because you are without a spare. Instead of being angry about missing the meeting, you focus on the fact that you can now call your grandmother while you are waiting for roadside assistance. The meeting can be rescheduled.

Grass only grows with rain. The rainbow comes after the storm. There is a gift in every perceived negative circumstance (problem) because we learn valuable life lessons through every experience.

It is imperative to address your happiness challenges with the happiness tools I introduce because this way you can maintain your happiness even in the face of adversity.

Use this happiness challenge tool

when bad things happen

so you can sustain your happiness

regardless of circumstances.

ACCEPTANCE MODEL

Bad things happen to all of us all the time.

Does this mean you are going to throw your happiness out of the window just because something happened you are unwilling to accept or like?

I am teaching you to develop a repertoire of tools you can use when bad things happen *so you can stay happy.*

So far you learned the Happiness Shield and Pollyanna's Game, and now I will teach you the Acceptance Model.

Use the Acceptance Model when

negative circumstances happen outside your control.

You may have heard of the serenity prayer before. This is a version of it except it is extremely pragmatic.

When something bad happens usually you react to it.

You are unable to believe that thing happened, that jerk hit your car, you were late on that payment, you just got fired... Whatever it is, that reactionary state is actually constricting your brain instead of expanding it.

Instead of reacting in the state that leads to the downward spiral, you must decide to do something different.

The **first** step of the Acceptance Model is *Choose to Accept.*

Everything starts with a decision. Before you get into the shower you decide to get into the shower. Before you get married you decide to get married. Before you do anything you make a decision to do it. In the Acceptance Model you make the decision to accept that that circumstance happened. Most likely it happened in the past so it is unable to be changed.

The **second** step is *Accept*; acceptance offers us emotional neutrality so we are able to think of how to handle the situation to the best of our ability. Acceptance is based on (1) the thing happened already and you are unable to change it, (2) faith that everything happens for a reason and something good may come of this, and (3) it is out of your control. This acceptance is powerful so we can move into the next step.

Step **three** is *Practical Response.* This means you have to handle the situation, regardless of what happens, you have to handle it. You are able to handle the situation like a cool, calm firefighter because you went through step two which is acceptance. By moving quickly into step three, you avoid the pitfalls of complaining.

Step **four** comes after you handle the circumstance. Take a minute to yourself.

Ask your heart, "What did I learn?"

Take a deep breath. Eyes are closed.

Put one hand on your heart and one hand on your belly.

Take another deep breath.

Drop your awareness into your heart center.

Focus your attention in the area of your heart.

Focus on creating an all loving, all nurturing, all accepting,

open environment there.

Then allow your heart beat to come through your chest to the palm of your hand.

When you can feel your heartbeat, ask yourself, to your heart,

"What did I learn?"

Wait for the response.

Ask, "Anything else?"

Repeat until your heart is complete.

Grass only grows with rain. The rainbow only comes after the storm.

Through the occurrence of negative circumstances we learn important lessons in life and move forward in our psychological and spiritual development. There could be multiple learnings in any given circumstance.

Step Five is Gratitude for the learning.

"I am grateful for_____(fill the blank with what your heart said in step four) because it adds _____ to my life."

Let's use a practical situation here. You step in dog poop.

Without the *Acceptance Model*: you yell, scream at the invisible dog owner, curse the invisible dog, throw a temper tantrum outside a busy restaurant, and ruin everyone's dinner. Anger, irritation, frustration, and embarrassment ensue.

With the Acceptance Model: you decide to accept that this happened. You take a deep breath, shrug your shoulders, and come into deep acceptance this is actually happening. You choose to practically respond by wiping off your shoe in nearby grass. You realize you learned you have to pay better attention to where you are walking. You are grateful for learning a lesson of being aware of where you are walking because it adds conscious awareness and mindfulness to your life. This results in a sweet smile, peace of heart, and peace of mind.

In which situation are you happier? One of my clients told me she had a bad day at work every day before she implemented the Acceptance Model.

Choosing acceptance as a way of life

removes the struggle and allows your life to

gently flow with ease around you.

Practice these tools every day for ninety days. There is a Protocol Sheet in Appendix A to help you overcome any challenges in life. Bankruptcy? Divorce? Hurricane? Chronic pain? Abuse? Business failure?

Whatever your challenge may be in life, there is an opportunity to overcome it by using the tools outlined in step three.

When faced with a challenge remember step one is to *choose happiness* above all else. Respond with *happiness*. Use the *tools* I taught you. Choose a *happiness booster* from step two to *boost* yourself back into a *positive mood!*

YOU CAN DO THIS!

LETTING GO AND FILLING UP MIND-BODY EXERCISE

This is a psychosomatic exercise that *aids in letting go.*

Psychosomatic means mind and body. When you have a thought, you can feel it in different areas of your body. There is a mind-body connection.

Many times throughout the day when faced with a challenge you feel a residual effect that you wish you could just let go. For example, you may get in an argument with the checkout cashier who is having a bad day, then get into your car, and snap at your daughter for zero reason. Then you realize it and feel badly until something good happens which gives you a positive mood boost. So, instead of carrying the 'yucky' feeling after an unpleasant experience, perform the Letting Go and Filling Up Exercise.

This exercise helps you let go of

residual negative feelings and

fills you up with positive, fulfilling feelings.

PREPARATION: WHAT ARE YOU READY TO LET GO OF?

Stand in a room alone where you will be undisturbed.

Put your arms next to your sides.

Take a deep breath.

Drop your awareness into your heart center.

Focus your attention in the area of your heart.

Focus on creating an all loving, all nurturing, all accepting,

open environment there.

Or, visualize yourself going to the airport to pick up someone you love

and use this memory to create that feeling inside.

Allow your heartbeat to come through your chest to the palm of your hand.

When you can feel your heartbeat, ask yourself,

"What am I ready to let go of?"

Wait for an answer.

When you hear the answer say,

"Is this the root issue?"

Wait for an answer.

Keep asking until you feel confident in what

your heart tells you are ready to let go.

For the sake of this exercise we use fear as the example.

PART A: LETTING GO EXERCISE

Put both your hands at your sides, close your eyes, and

take a deep breath.

Drop your awareness into your heart center

Focus your attention in the area of your heart.

Focus on creating an all loving, all nurturing,

all accepting, open environment.

Go back to the first memory of fear,

second memory of fear,

third memory of fear,

fourth memory of fear,

fifth memory of fear,

*all the while **concentrating on the feeling of fear** in your body.*

Visualize it coming from the

depths of your soul to the surface of your skin.

Continue flipping through your memory banks like a rolodex,

never staying too long *at each memory.*

Visualize the feeling of fear moving

through your arms to your hands

and through your legs to your feet

so your whole body feels all consumed with this feeling of fear.

When you feel current in your memory banks

and every single cell is feeling fear,

then take a deep breath.

Raise your hands above your head,

and put your middle fingers together

with your palms facing down toward the ground.

Press down the front of your body in concert with your exhale,

brushing your index finger against your body

as you press down all the way to the ground.

Stand up, and place one hand on your heart.

Ask yourself, to your heart,

"Do I need to repeat that exercise?"

Wait for a response.

If you need to repeat this exercise, go ahead.

The next time you may have different memories.

This is a method of peeling the onion of memories.

You may have multiple layers of fear.

Do it as many times as your heart guides you.

Repeat that exercise until your heart is complete.

Then move on to Part B: The Filling Up Exercise.

PART B: THE FILLING UP EXERCISE

This Filling Up Exercise is Part B as the Letting Go Exercise is Part A.

You are going to **fill up with the opposite** of what you just let go.

In this case the opposite of fear is faith and trust.

Put your hands at your sides with eyes closed.

Take a deep breath.

Drop your awareness into your heart center.

Focus your attention in the area of your heart.

Focus on cultivating a natural light feeling of faith in your heart.

You may feel a sense of freedom, peace, serenity, tranquility, and calm.

Cultivate those feelings of peace, faith, trust, acceptance, tranquility, and

serenity, only focusing on those feelings in your heart
with an absence of thought.

Visualize these feelings getting stronger and stronger,
warmer and warmer, fuzzier and fuzzier.

Visualize these feelings moving through

your arms to your hands,

through your legs to your feet.

When you feel like every single cell in your body is filled with faith,

take a deep breath, raise your hands above your head,

and spread your arms wide above you.

Visualize connecting into the universe around you to get all of the faith.

When you feel that connection,

put your middle fingers together and

press down the front of your body in concert with your exhale.

This time visualizing filling up from head to toe

as you press down the front of your body,

brushing your index finger against your body

as you go all the way to the ground.

Again you are visualizing filling up and

letting in the faith from head to toe.

Feels so good!

Then stand up and take a deep breath.

Put your hand on your heart. Ask yourself, to your heart, "Do I need to repeat that exercise?"

Wait for a response.

Follow the guidance of your heart.

When your heart is complete, there you have it: the Letting Go and Filling Up Exercise.

Letting Go of the Old, Bringing in the New

You can do this exercise for anything you are ready to let go of: a relationship, a habit, an issue, or a recurring negative thought. Whatever it is, even if you get into a fight with someone else and you have that unshakable angry feeling afterward, you can do the exercise.

Feel completely different

in a matter of minutes

TIMING

The timing for the Letting Go and Filling Up Exercise is as follows:

Ask your heart, "What am I ready to let go of?" = one to three minutes depending on how long it takes to get into your heart space and identify with clarity and confidence the accurate issue.

Letting Go Exercise = two minutes to ten minutes depending on how many times your heart instructs you to repeat the exercise.

Filling Up Exercise = two minutes to ten minutes depending how many times your heart guides you to repeat the exercise.

TOTAL AMOUNT OF TIME FOR

THE LETTING GO AND FILLING UP EXERCISE

— between 4 minutes and 23 minutes

STEP 3 MASTERY

In summary, between using your Happiness Shield, Pollyanna's Game, the Acceptance Model, and the Letting Go and Filling Up Exercise, I am confident you can keep your happiness in the face of adversity.

There is zero way anything can

overcome your sustainable happiness.

By using the tools I have provided, you will be able to knock happiness challenges out of the park and continue on your upward spiral! Your resiliency could increase from days to minutes using these tools.

Magic and rainbows,

here you come!

CHAPTER 6: CONTENTMENT

STEP 4 - FOLLOW YOUR HEART

Before going into step four, I recommend keeping with the first three steps for a while until you get the hang of it. Practice for a few weeks to really build a solid foundation of empowerment, positive mood, and resiliency. The last two steps are considered ADVANCED HAPPINESS, and the others are needed as a prerequisite to be able to truly access pure eudaimonia and chaironic happiness after you build a strong foundation.

When you feel confident in walking in your upward spiral of steps one through three on your own, then your foundation is strong enough for steps four and five.

You have been doing great!

You are learning how to control your own happiness, boost your mood whenever you like, and at this point zero happiness challenges are too difficult for you. Your happiness is like a marathon; those challenges become mere hurdles, and you leap over one right after the other with ease and flow.

Where are you going? What is next in your happiness?

Let's see if you are ready to move on the advanced happiness class of eudaimonia: deep inner contentment and fulfillment.

POP QUIZ

1. Do you feel empowered over your own happiness?

2. Do you know techniques to boost your mood whenever you want?

3. Are you overcoming adversity with great leaps and big smiles?

If you answered yes to all of the questions above, then you can proceed on to the next two levels in happiness. Eudaimonic and chaironic happiness await you! I want to be extremely clear: I recommend moving forward only if you feel mastership over your own happiness, positive mood, and resiliency.

Eudaimonia is the deeper conversation. Unlike hedonic happiness, eudaimonic happiness takes time to develop. The hedonic happiness bursts (zestful joy) you get from your "I am happy!" jumps fade away fast whereas eudaimonic happiness requires more of a time investment. It feels like a quiet contentment and a warm inner peace in your heart. It is the difference between discontent and content, emptiness and fulfillment, or shallowness and depth. It is a feeling in which you are covered with a warm blanket, have the strength of an ox, and possess an open, pure, and loving heart. When you have developed eudaimonia in your soul you have peace of mind.

Without eudaimonia you have discontentment, confusion, and emptiness. You experience a lack of meaning and purpose in your life. You are totally out of touch with who you are let alone being actualized in the world. You are on a crusade to fix your problems because there are so many. Your heart feels like a burned out, empty, decrepit brick building-worn and torn.

In eudaimonia, you are content and fulfilled. You feel as if you are a tranquil pond and have a strong sense of meaning and purpose in life. You are in touch with your true, inner soul as well as accepting and confident in who you are. You are using your strengths every day in every way. Your heart feels open, loving, peaceful, strong, confident, and uplifted... like a rose garden.

EU-DAIMON-IC

EU- is good, DAIMON is spirit, -IC is nature of

The exercises outlined in this chapter focus on developing deep inner contentment in your heart center. This is soul development which is needed to access this level of contentment inside your heart. It will take a long time to complete these exercises, and that is ok because contentment takes awhile to develop. It is a journey just like taking control of your own happiness, learning how to build a positive mood, or mastering resiliency when faced with challenges.

I assure you this work will lead you to develop a deep level of contentment and fulfillment in your heart.

You may notice that you will still experience negative emotions while you have achieved contentment. The difference being that you are now in control of your emotional experience so you can choose to experience the natural emotions for up to ninety seconds. Then you can decide what is in your best interest in that moment. Maybe it is appropriate to choose to experience grief due to the loss of a loved one. You can choose happiness when you are ready, yet you understand and accept that waves of grief are a part of your human experience.

This enables you to embrace your human experience

yet master your emotional experience.

You are in control of your emotional experience instead of your emotional experience being in control of you. You can still engage with your MAPS in life and feel content and fulfilled while having emotional experiences appropriate to your circumstances.

HEART BASED MAPS

Your heart based MAPS (meaning, authenticity, purpose, and strengths) lead you to a deep inner contentment, a sense of fulfillment, and a simple warmth inside.

You likely thought you will get this feeling when you get the right person, place, thing, or circumstance in your life. This is false. Something external to you is absolutely unable to make your heart warm, content, and fulfilled.

This is something that must be developed from your inner experience. This is a shift in the pursuit of happiness from the external to the internal. A feeling of emptiness turns into fulfillment once you connect from your heart to your MAPS.

HEART AND MIND

The difference between your heart and your mind is a crucial lesson in happiness because you will never achieve deep inner contentment, a sense of fulfillment, and achieve states of bliss and joy *in your mind*.

Contentment is in your heart,

and bliss is in your soul.

You can create this eudaimonia through the guidance of your heart's wisdom. When you both tune in to your heart and, as Steven Adler, M.S., D.D. (Doctor of Divinity), also known as 'Sacred Steve' says, "Train your mind to become a willing servant of your heart," you are able to achieve peace of mind, deep inner contentment, and fulfillment.

Your mind is processing a lot! You are a smart being and with that intelligence comes eleven different categories of self awareness: values, beliefs, thoughts about myself, emotions, capabilities, unique talents, strengths, motives, desires, purpose, and goals.

Intelligence comes with a conscious and subconscious mind, different cultural influences, societal, parental, media, and religious influences.

You can think of multiple answers to multiple questions at any given time. Your mind is trained for analytics. When it comes to deep inner contentment, it is unable to figure out what to do.

Because of the nature of the mind, it is thinking about something in the future or something in the past. It is never satisfied with the moment and needs to be in action, engaging in accomplishment. The mind is rarely engaged with the flow in this moment.

Only when you are *being* in your heart twenty-four hours a day, seven days a week, can you create peace of mind where you actually will stop all of that thinking. In other words, contentment helps quiet your mind.

You are able to speak from your heart, and wisdom comes at all times. You can transcend thinking altogether and simply focus on *being*. It is in this *being* state that we achieve deep inner contentment.

Yet we have to *be* engaged in our MAPS. *Thinking* our MAPS is a different experience than *being* our MAPS. Human *doing*. Human *thinking*. Human *being*. Which one are you? Human *being!* Again, it is only when you are being your MAPS that you are able to experience eudaimonia.

Let's do an exercise that will show you, with your own heart and mind, the difference between the voice in your heart and the voice in your mind.

Get a piece of paper and a pencil. I am going to ask you a question, and I want you to write down the answer of whatever quickly comes to mind. The question is, "What did you do today?"

Write down all the things that arose. What did you do?

OK, you have written down everything you have done today on a piece of paper. Now I am going to guide you into your heart space.

I am going to ask you a question, and you are going to repeat the question to yourself. Wait for the response to come from your heart.

This is going to be a self-meditative state, and you have been doing this throughout the book. Make sure you are in a room by yourself and will be undisturbed.

Put both feet on the ground.

Close your eyes.

Place one hand on your heart and one hand on your belly.

Take a deep breath, one more time for good measure.

Drop your awareness into your heart center.

Focus your attention in the area of your heart.

Focus on creating an all loving, all nurturing, all accepting,

open environment there.

Then allow your heartbeat to come through your chest

to the palm of your hand.

When you can feel your heartbeat, ask yourself, to your heart,

"What did I do today?"

Wait for the response.

When the response comes, ask,

"Anything else?"

Continue to ask for anything else until your heart is complete.

When you are ready, you can bring your awareness back to the here and now.

There are often different answers

between your heart and your mind

to the same question.

The mind gave answers off your to-do list: I showered, I ate, I went to work, I paid the bills, I drove here... very action and accomplishment oriented.

Whereas your heart brought a different level of experience into the inquiry which had more to do with the feelings, relationships, the senses, the meaning behind all the actions and accomplishments, and a perspective of a deeper sense of what it means to be a human being.

Instead of connecting to your MAPS through your mind you have to connect through your heart.

For instance, you would be connecting through your mind if your parents were lawyers, and they told you your purpose was to be a lawyer. However, if your heart really wanted to be working in Africa helping underprivileged students at a school, you would be discontented and unfulfilled because you are planning on going to law school. Until you follow your heart, you will find emptiness and turmoil - the opposite of peace and contentment.

If you never follow your heart,

you will never fully achieve

EUDAIMONIA.

When it comes to important questions like:

What is my life purpose?

Who am I?

What are my strengths?

The answers must come from your heart space instead of your mind.

HEART SPACE

Heart space is terminology used to describe a self-meditative state where you focus on listening to the voice in your heart.

You can access this voice for anything at all, whether it is a question about if you might wear the red pants or blue pants, get married to certain someone, or plan a career. Whatever it is, your heart always has an answer.

Sit by yourself. Take a deep breath.

Eyes are closed with feet on the ground.

Put one hand on your heart, one hand on your belly.

Take another deep breath, and one more breath for good measure.

Drop your awareness into your heart center.

Focus your attention into the area of your heart.

Focus on creating an all loving, all nurturing, all accepting,

open environment there.

Allow your heartbeat to come through your chest

to the palm of your hand.

When you can feel your heartbeat, ask yourself

whatever question you want to your heart.

Wait for the answer.

I recommend asking anything else until your heart is complete.

One daily practice that I recommend to people is to ask your heart, "Where am I on the happiness scale 1-10?"

Wait for an answer.

If your heart is less than a 10, ask,

"What do I need in order to be a 10?"

Wait for an answer.

"Anything else?"

Repeat until your heart is complete.

This becomes your part of your advanced happiness action plan for the day. I recommend you add it to your morning routine after the gratitude practice.

You can keep track each day to see exactly how long you are able to sustain your happiness.

To cultivate your deepest eudaimonia, you need to access your deepest heart's MAPS. MAPS is an acronym for meaning, authenticity, purpose, and strengths. In this program we focus primarily on your strengths and authenticity. We have found your purpose in life lies within your authenticity, and your meaning in life lies within your purpose. Each person has a unique purpose in life, and each person will derive a sense of meaning individuated to your own inner heart strings based on previous life experiences. In this process, we will focus most attention on the S and the A of the MAPS as the purpose and meaning are found within the exercises we do for authenticity.

STRENGTHS

We begin with the strengths even though it is at the end of the MAPS since it is the easiest, helps boost your self-esteem, and creates positive social bonds with your closest relationships.

There are a couple of ways you can identify your strengths. The first method used is the 'VIA Survey of Character Strengths' which is a scientific assessment devised by Dr. Chris Peterson of the University of Michigan and Dr. Martin Seligman of the University of Pennsylvania. VIA stands for Values In Action. This survey is the opposite of the DSM manual which is the disorder manual psychologists use to diagnose disorders. Instead of telling you what is wrong with you, psychology can now tell you what is great about you!

Get comfortable and sit down in front of the computer to take this particular strengths test. Have your tea ready because it will take a good forty minutes. I recommend you take the 240-question survey instead of the short one to determine your character strengths. When you are finished with the test, memorize your top five strengths so you can use them in the face of adversity and every outlet of your life. It is important you have outlets for your strengths daily.

Register a free account at www.authentichappiness.com to take the test.

Another method to determine your strengths is called the Reflected Best Self Exercise (RBSE) which originated at the University of Michigan Business School (every single MBA student needs to get through this exercise in order to graduate). The method used for this assessment involves email communication. I recommend that you do this for currently $75 on the ReflectedBestSelfExercise.com website or search for "Reflected Best Self Exercise".

The purpose of both assessments is to cross validate the value of the answers between you and your community as well as gain an understanding of your unique strength-based context. For you to feel the greatest amount of eudaimonia, you must use your strengths on a daily basis.

Also, it is important to develop the happiness strengths of kindness, love, optimism, and zest.

MY HAPPY SELF

It is time to meet your happy self!

This exercise is based in the eleven categories of self awareness: values, beliefs, thoughts about myself, emotions, capabilities, unique talents, strengths, motives, desires, purpose, and goals.

The "My Happy Self" exercise is the meat of your MAPS specifically the authenticity portion.

Authenticity is owning and acting

in accordance with your true self.

Most people are lost when it comes to the deeper question of "Who am I?"

This exercise has a Part A and Part B. Part A helps with the first part of authenticity: 'owning'. Part B helps with the second part of authenticity: 'acting'.

PART A

Get a piece of paper and a pencil and write down these eleven categories:

values, beliefs, emotions, thoughts about myself, capabilities, unique talents, desires, motives, strengths, purpose, and goals.

Underneath, write "What is the _____ of my happy self?"

Fill in the blank with values, beliefs, emotions, etc. First, you need to guide yourself into your heart space. Make sure you are able to be by yourself where you will be undisturbed.

Close your eyes, and take a deep breath.

Take another breath for good measure.

Drop your awareness into your heart center.

Focus your attention in the area of your heart.

Focus on creating an all loving, all nurturing, all accepting,

open environment there.

When this has been achieved, allow your heartbeat to come

through your chest to the palm of your hand.

When you can feel your heartbeat, ask yourself, to your heart,

"What are the values of my happy self?"

Wait for the response.

Ask, " Anything else?"

Continue to ask for anything else until your heart is complete.

Now get a recording device. Record yourself during this exercise. Go into your heart space, ask the question about one of the eleven categories, and repeat your heart's answers out loud.

Then after you have come out of your heart space, transcribe the recording. Take your time. I recommend only doing two or three categories in a day until you complete it. Each category could take about ten or fifteen minutes. Remember that contentment takes time to develop. You are going to have to put some time into this exercise. You have to invest in your own inner peace by making time to listen to your heart's answers to the most important question of all: "Who am I?"

For the overachievers, I recommend making an art piece similar to the Desiderata, a 1927 inspirational prose poem by American writer Max Ehrmann. Make the text come alive through a creative self expression.

You can use this in your introduction or make copies and pass it out to your community when you introduce your new happy self!

Sometimes it can be nerve wracking coming into authenticity with those you love. You have to push through those nerves and do it anyway!

PART B

After you are done with Part A, you are going to identify your ten closest relationships and introduce your happy self to those ten people. Preferably in person, by video chat, or a phone call. Present to one person at a time if you can. Feel confident and excited to unveil the real you!

After you have introduced your happy self to those ten people you are going to feel a BURST of eudaimonic happiness inside, a burst of deep inner contentment, a sense of fulfillment, and a warming sensation in your heart.

This is due to the engagement of your MAPS. You found out the answers of who you were meant to be (owning) and introduced yourself to your loved ones (acting). In the moment owning and acting connect through the bonds of your ten close relationships, your eudaimonia strengthens.

As long as you continue to engage in your MAPS and actualize your happy self from your heart for every moment of every day, you will feel eudaimonia. This is sustainable. This means you are your authentic self, you are using your strengths, and you are accomplishing your life's purpose which gives you a great sense of meaning in life.

It seems easy, OK sure, just ask your heart some questions, get some answers, tell some people about it, and then you are sustainably happy?

It seems too easy?!

This is because authenticity appears to be an easy thing, yet to do it may be an ideal for which we are constantly striving.

It could be an ideal because there are 48 known barriers that can occur within our psychology that will lead us away from authenticity in any given moment. My doctoral research identified these 48 known barriers.

This is a lot of stop signs you have to go through in order to claim being totally authentic. This appears to be a simple idea, yet it is more complex than you can imagine. See Appendix B for a table reference of these barriers where you can learn about the barriers in your own self-awareness that direct you away from authenticity and, consequently, away from your happiness.

Like happiness, authenticity is something that can be learned.

One day, I was thrilled to receive a call from a teaching assistant at Stanford who told me they wanted to use my doctoral research of the 48 barriers in their Social Emotional class! That day, I had a call with one of my mentors, and he started laughing and was unable to believe we were at a point in society where we have to teach and learn authenticity (especially at a Stanford level of education).

TIMING FOR STEP 4

Adding ask your heart, "Where am I on the happiness scale? What do I need to be a 10?" = 1 minute in the morning routine

Strengths Identification (VIA + Best Self) = 1 hour

Happy Self Exercise Part A = 5 hours (+1 hour for creative expression)

Happy Self Exercise Part B = 11 hours

Total hours to develop contentment = 18 hours

Total = 18 hours to develop inner contentment!

STEP 4 MASTERY

You have mastered the art of contentment when you are totally aware of your heart based MAPS, and you are actualizing them in every moment of every day. You know you have mastered contentment and fulfillment when you have developed a pure, warm inner peace in your heart center.

When nothing can take you away from actualizing your MAPS, you have developed contentment. When you are fully engaged with your MAPS, every moment you have achieved sustainable happiness with eudaimonia.

When you experience the range of human emotions yet still feel content inside, you have mastered step four.

CHAPTER 6: BLISS

STEP 6 - BLISS AND JOY

You have come a long way. You have learned how to take charge of your own happiness, create a positive mood whenever you want, you are resilient with challenges, and you are developing inner contentment and fulfillment. What is next?!

BLISS AND JOY!

We had to build up to this.

We had to be able to create a strong happiness foundation for you to reach this advanced state of happiness where we can feel exuberant, effervescent elation any time you want.

This is chaironic happiness. This type of happiness comes from the connection to something greater than yourself: albeit, God, the universe, nature, or whatever it is for you. It is achieved through visits in nature, Reiki healings and attunements, meditation, church and so forth.

I encourage you to keep a magic and rainbows journal of all of the things that happen on a daily basis that would indicate you are part of a whole. These are things like seeing a heart-shaped cloud in the sky, being asked by a stranger the very thing you were thinking about earlier, and flowing in your time experience. This is overall harmony in your life when everything is perfect... even the rain.

When you have achieved deeper contentment and are experiencing states of bliss and joy, there is a peace of mind and a peace of heart. Your life is in flow perfectly with your life path.

You arrive at the right place at the right time, talk to the right people, and say the right things. You are doing exactly what you were meant to do on your life path. When you can feel these highest of high states, the sky's the limit. You are able to be the biggest and brightest versions of yourself. You are able to honor the divinity in life and in yourself.

Back to step one: The Happiness Decision.

Remember when it seemed impossible to make The Happiness Decision? Remember when you felt like happiness was egotistical, self-centered, shallow, and far from worth the weight you put on it?

This is an opportunity for you to be

the peace you want to see for others.

This is your opportunity to show up for people in a way that feels good to them and to yourself. This is a way for you to contribute happiness and health to those around you.

It truly starts with step one of The Happiness Decision.

So now you are convinced that your happiness is in your control.

Step five is the icing on the cake.

It is what you have been waiting for.

It is a lightness of being, a smile on your face and in your heart, a consistent warm and fuzzy feeling, inner ox-like strength, unwavering acceptance, confidence, and gratitude for every breath.

Pure love,

peaceful bliss,

and effervescent joy

in your heart

This feeling is the experience of bliss. I will introduce three types of bliss: effervescent bliss, light bliss, and peaceful divine bliss.

EFFERVESCENT BLISS

You have already experienced it through jumping for joy with five "I am happy!" jumps. Do it right now, just for the joy of it! Jump up for effervescent bliss, and exclaim, "I am happy!" five times!

Let's do some right now to get started. Put one hand in the air, jump up, and say, "I am happy!"

"I am happy! I am happy! I am happy! I am happy! I am happy!"

YES!

Effervescent Bliss!

Whew!

LIGHT BLISS

Light bliss is a feeling derived from the choice of faith where faith means trust. If you put out positive you get back positive - that is right!

Many unhappy people project fear when thinking about the future and regret when reflecting on the past. Choose faith over fear when you are faced with the unknown. This is trusting in the divine path of your life.

Step five addresses spirituality at some level.

For those of you who are having a difficult time considering faith as a spiritual concept, think about faith as trust in yourself. Trust in yourself to be able to identify a realistic goal, have an achievable plan, and the belief in yourself to achieve it. For the other people who are more spiritually inclined, think about faith as connecting to something larger than yourself.

Good things do unfold in front of us all the time. When faced with the unknown, you have the option of choosing faith or fear.

You are creating your current state

from a perception in the moment.

You can always choose a different perception,

one that is empowering for you and will be helpful to you.

You may be consciously or subconsciously choosing fear when faced with the unknown.

Instead of letting fear creep in for an unbeknownst reason, consciously choose faith in the future and trust things are going to work out for your highest good.

Let's use a real life example. Picture the traffic you will have to deal with after work... fear it is going to be bad.

Now choose faith. Picture the traffic moving easily and quickly, and you get home before your normal time. This is because you had faith to determine a new route.

Which one felt better?

Faith, of course.

This is a feeling of light bliss.

You can have trust in yourself by choosing faith over fear.

If you are having a difficult time choosing faith over fear, go back to weeding this aspect out of your garden of happiness.

Consider what Louise Hay says, "Out of this situation only good will come."

We have to choose faith over fear

every time we are faced with the unknown.

This will lead us into states of bliss and joy

beyond our wildest dreams!

PEACEFUL DIVINE BLISS

The next method for achieving a state of peaceful divine bliss is by connecting with the divine through emptiness.

Do this meditation with me. It will just take a few moments of your time.

Close your eyes, take a deep breath, and sit comfortably.

Take another deep breath and relax.

Picture a chalkboard.

Put all of your thoughts on the chalkboard.

When they are all on the chalkboard, erase them.

Draw a dot in the center of the board.

Concentrate on the dot.

Honor the remaining thoughts.

See them dissipate, and let them go.

Feel your emotions honor them.

See them dissipate, and let them go.

Feel your physical sensations. Honor them.

See them dissipate, and let them go.

Again, see your thoughts dissipate and let them go.

See your emotions dissipate, and let them go.

Feel your physical sensations, and let them go.

Zero thoughts, zero emotions, and zero physical sensations.

Go through this process until you feel an emptiness.

When you notice you are feeling emptiness,

put the corners of your mouth toward your cheekbones.

Hold that position for as long as you like.

There you have it: Peaceful Divine Bliss.

You took away your human experience of thoughts, emotions, and physical sensations so you were able to reach a peaceful feeling of emptiness and divine connection.

Part of your positive psychology practice is to adopt faith based practices:

1. *Choose faith over fear*

2. *Meditate*

3. *Join a spiritual organization*

4. *Frequent visits to nature*

5. *Keep a Magic and Rainbows Journal when you notice serendipity*

6. *Practice emptiness*

7. *Study Reiki*

TIMING FOR STEP 5

Jumping Up for Joy = 50 seconds / 5 times a day

Choosing Faith over Fear = 2 seconds

Meditating into Emptiness = 150 seconds / 5 times a day

Total Time for Step Five = 3.36 Minutes!

You can experience a sense of joy and bliss practically at the blink of an eye. Although just like the first four steps, you have to practice with persistence, and the more you practice, the deeper your joy and more peaceful your bliss.

STEP 5 MASTERY

When people have nothing, they have faith. When people are faced with the most horrific of life's circumstances is when people turn to God in whatever form you know it to be.

Everyone is faced with the unknown. If you were to embrace that you are living a divine life, one granted to you by the divine will and grace of God, you would be appreciating everything, even your breath. You would feel taken care of by Mother Earth and the grace of God like you are living in a divine golden egg of nurturance.

When you can hold a sense of faith while on your deathbed, receiving terrible news, losing everything, having nothing, or experiencing 'rock bottom', things turn around.

This belief in a higher power or a connection to something greater than yourself allows you to put your ego aside and live in the service of helping others. Life is about more than just you. It is about your service in helping others. This overwhelming sense of confidence and security in your life's purpose gives you the strength of an ox to persevere through tough times and the lightness of being it takes when merged as one with the divine in times of adversity. It gives you the ability to have compassion for those who are in deep suffering.

When you know your mind is a calm, tranquil pond and you are feeling the wholeness of pure love, effervescent joy, and peaceful bliss in your heart and soul during times of crisis, trauma, pain, and chaos, you have mastered step five.

CHAPTER 7: SUSTAINABLE HAPPINESS

MASTERING ALL 5 STEPS

When you have mastery of all 5 steps you will get interviewed for the nightly news! I am joking! Well, maybe? I was interviewed on CBS about teaching the Happiness Makeover® and the results that positive psychology can bring to your life.

In the meantime, find assurance within yourself that happiness is a practice just like anything. You are starting a learning curve, and it takes time to develop mastery of all five steps. This is a moment to moment experience. Are you constantly empowered over your own happiness? Are you constantly engaging in happiness-boosting activities? Are you constantly using these tools to overcome your happiness challenges? Are you constantly engaged in your MAPS (meaning, authenticity, purpose, and strengths)? Are you constantly choosing faith over fear?

If you want a happier life, I have outlined many step-by-step processes for you to implement so you can see results fast. Now it is up to you to put this into practice.

The first step is a one-time experience of thirty minutes, the second step is eight minutes of daily practice, the third step is on average ten minutes of daily practice, the fourth step is eighteen hours, and the fifth step is three minutes and 35 seconds of daily practice. Minus the one-time activities, the happiness practice I am encouraging you to engage in is a total of 21 minutes and 35 seconds every day.

Do you have approximately twenty minutes a day to devote to your happiness?! Of course you do!

For those people who are already happy and want to teach other people how to be happy, do you know how to take your upward spiral even beyond these five steps? Share your happiness with others! Your happiness impacts up to three degrees of separation of every single person you come into contact with so do you want your family to be happier? Do you want your office to be happier? Do you want the neighborhood school kids to be happier? How can you bring this cutting edge information into your family, friends, and community?

Here are ways you can take your sustainable happiness to the next level:

1. Check out new offerings at www.HappinessforHumanKind.com.
2. Share this book with someone you love.
3. If you want to look into happiness in your profession, I recommend my "Blissful Calling Workbook".
4. Start a Happiness Club.

Beyond the inspiration of taking yourself to the next level in your happiness, I think it is fitting to further inspire you into action with a quote about the true meaning of life:

"We are visitors on this planet. We are here for ninety or one hundred years at the very most. During that period, we must try to do something good, something useful, with our lives. If you contribute to other people's happiness, you will find the true goal, the true meaning of life."

                                        - His Holiness, the 14th Dalai Lama

CHAPTER 8: INTEGRATIVE APPROACH

WHAT IS AN INTEGRATIVE APPROACH?

Many people in positive psychology are recognizing the need to address all parts of our humanity - mind, body, and spirit.

When all three areas of your life are addressed, change is inevitable. When you just focus on one or another part, then the results that can be gained from addressing the self as a cohesive system is lost.

I know some of you may just want to incorporate the mind portion or the body portion or maybe just the spirit portion of this transformative process. Yet I know the results that are possible because I see them unfold in front of my face every day. I see the union of mind, body, and spirit in each person, as each part of us is just as important.

When considering this approach to happiness, consider incorporating all aspects of your being - mind, body, and spirit.

BODY - ISAGENIX NUTRITION TECHNOLOGY

Isagenix means 'balanced life' in Latin. It is a very sophisticated, all natural nutrition technology used in the Happiness Makeover® for proper nutrients, cleansing toxicity from the body, and balancing brain chemistry. It can also help with weight loss, which is totally optional for your Makeover.

The Isagenix program has multiple components like any other technology. First thing in the morning, drink a shake comprised of every single nutrient your body requires for optimal functioning. The ingredients of the shake are based in raw food. It has a different drink for cleansing toxicity from the body on a cellular level. This is a molecular cleanse. This is different from a liver cleanse or a colon cleanse; it is literally going to clean every cell in your body.

The fundamental philosophy behind incorporating Isagenix products for the body component of the Happiness Makeover® is to address the problem you are likely without getting enough nutrients in your day-to-day meals. As a consequence, your body is lacking the basic nutrition it needs in order to function optimally. You may be surviving in a nutritionally bankrupt, toxic environment breathing, drinking, and showering in toxins daily. There are over 200 toxins that we come into contact with every single day.

In the Happiness Makeover® I get peace of mind to know my clients are getting the nutrients they need for optimal bodily functioning. They are actively releasing the toxicity from their body and balancing their brain chemistry through proper mineral consumption. Some people choose to consciously lose weight during their makeover, too, and combined with daily exercise, the results can be outstanding!

I have seen dramatic and lasting results for myself and others using Isagenix products since 2006. Start by reading about it at https://happinessdoctor.isagenix.com to learn more. The benefits I have seen include happiness, mental clarity, more energy, better overall health, and weight loss.

SPIRIT - REIKI ENERGY HEALING

When an unhappy person walks into a room at a party, someone often scowls and says, "Don't look over there, look who arrived..." When a happy person walks in the room at a party, someone often says, "Who is that?! Introduce me!"

This is simply based on the energy of the person. This person has said nothing yet is either giving off 'good vibes' or 'bad vibes'.

People can feel this energetic transference all day long. The scientific terminology is emotional contagion. When you feel bad, other people feel bad around you, and when you feel good, others feel good around you.

Eckhart Tolle talks about the pain body and how we consistently want to relinquish our pain body to anyone who will take it. After you get in a fight with someone, that uneasy feeling still stays with you for some time.

Someone who has experienced a lot of unhappiness in their life has experienced a lot of pain and suffering and is holding on to the energetic pain from each individual experience. This is referred to as cellular memory patterns. If we almost get in an accident or we do get in an accident, that memory will be with us until we do something about it.

In the Happiness Makeover®, Reiki has helped people heal from painful experiences of the past so they can move forward in life in a new and positive way.

Reiki is a form of energy healing based on symbols that works with the chakra system in the body. If you have attended a yoga class you may have heard of the several chakras (energy centers) we have in our body. Each chakra represents different things in our lives including survival, security, self-esteem, love, communication, intuition, and spirituality.

Reiki is what Jesus and Buddha did to heal with their hands. It is a tradition that has been used for thousands of years in Tibetan Buddhism to achieve enlightenment.

It has a spiritual background, yet Reiki has been studied by the National Institute of Health and used by the United States Army to treat Post Traumatic Stress Disorder (PTSD). It has also been used for hospice patients, in oncology wards, and during surgeries. Dr. Oz has endorsed it, and it is currently being used on healing-oriented television shows.

As of 2018, there are about 500 peer-reviewed journal articles discussing Reiki and the healing benefits it offers. For example, Reiki helps in recovering from illness faster, stress reduction, relaxation, and aids in treating depression and anxiety.

In 2006, I began incorporating Reiki energy into the Happiness Makeover® to account for the spirit component of the mind-body-spirit approach. Each client becomes a student of Reiki and learns how to use it for their own self-healing.

There is a sacred ceremony performed by a Reiki Master where there is a transference of the sacred healing Reiki symbols to the student. There are different levels to this healing method: level one (healing the heart), level two (emotional healing), and level three (healing the soul). Each of the three makeover months highlight a new level of healing. At the moment of an attunement, a spiritual purification process goes underway, and the student begins a journey of subconscious healing. This healing process addresses suffering in the subconscious by healing the heart, emotional healing, and healing the soul on all levels - mentally, emotionally, physically, and spiritually.

Reiki aids in healing your subconscious wounds by clearing and healing your chakra system.

Once a student undergoes an attunement (passing of the symbols from a Reiki Master) then a 21-day chakra cleanse begins where the Reiki energy cleans, heals, and purifies each chakra for three days at a time.

Reiki works on spiritual, mental, emotional, and physical

levels and transcends time and space.

The healing that occurs for people during the three 21-day chakra cleanses is astounding. Many different symptoms can occur during this time. Students are given a sheet which outlines the symptoms and makes recommendations to counter the symptoms during their Reiki chakra cleanse.

Students experience serendipity every day where they are seeing how their inside experience is affecting their outer experiences in life.

Real life examples of what my students experienced with serendipitous healing while in the 21-day chakra cleanse included:

> **Survival**: A Last Will and Testament was discussed.
>
> **Security**: Keys to a safe were lost.
>
> **Self-Esteem**: External validation was received.
>
> **Love**: Three exes called in three days, and these relationships were mended.
>
> **Communication**: A student who was holding something in and without communicating to another person in ten years suddenly experienced a call from that person within the three days, and the thing the student had been holding in effortlessly came forth.
>
> **Intuition**: An insight into an experience arrived before the experience occurred.
>
> **Spirituality**: Feelings of connecting to something greater than oneself and wanting to help others developed.

Students are recommended to be deeply aware of themselves during the cleansing process especially by observing their thoughts, conversations, dreams, and experiences as it relates to each chakra.

Being attuned to Reiki energy and being given the ability to self-heal aids in developing chaironic happiness: spiritual joy and bliss.

Chaironic happiness offers you states of bliss and joy when you feel connected to something greater than yourself.

In brief, the Reiki portion of the Happiness Makeover® helps heal the subconscious, empowers self-healing, builds faith, and aids in developing chaironic happiness (Step 5: states of bliss and joy).

CHAPTER 9: TRANSFORMATION

CONCLUSION

Your life changed when you learned how to tie your shoes.

Your life changed when you learned how to read.

Your life changed when you learned math.

Your life changed when you learned how to use happiness science.

Your life changed when you learned how to control your mood.

Your life changed when you learned how to become a positive thinker.

Your life changed when you learned how to overcome challenges.

Your life changed when you learned how to access your heart's voice.

Your life changed when you learned your heart's life purpose.

Your life changed when you discovered your true authentic self.

Your life changed when you realized your strengths.

Your life changed when you learned to choose faith over fear.

Your life changed when you learned how to jump for joy.

Your life changed when you learned emptiness.

Your life will change

more rapidly and more powerfully

when you incorporate

Isagenix Nutrition Technology and Reiki Energy

into your journey to

Sustainable Happiness.

This life change will lead you into the upward spiral of your dreams.

You have inner peace of mind and heart, you are smiling and laughing every day, your relationships are flourishing, your health is better than ever, you are making more money than ever, and you will live at least 7 years longer.

Everything is better when you are happy!

If it takes you every day for the rest of your life to perfect this positive psychology in practice program, it is worth it.

This is the most important work of your life.

REFERENCES

Abbe, A., Tkach, C., & Lyubomirsky, S. (2003). The art of living by dispositionally happy people. *Journal of Happiness Studies, 4,* 385-404.

Achor, S. (2010). The happiness advantage: The seven principles of positive psychology that fuel success and performance at work. New York: Crown Publishing.

Ben-Shahar, T. (2007) Happier: Learn the secrets to daily joy and lasting fulfillment. New York: McGraw-Hill Education.

Biswas-Diener, R. & Dean, B. (2007). Positive psychology coaching: Putting the science of happiness to work for your clients. Hoboken: John Wiley & Sons, Inc.

Biswas-Diener, R. (2010). Practicing positive psychology coaching: Assessment, activities, and strategies for success. Hoboken: John Wiley & Sons, Inc.

Blankson, A. & Achor S. (2017). The future of happiness: 5 modern strategies for balancing productivity and well-being in the digital era. Dallas: BenBella Books.

Boehm, J. K., Lyubomirsky, S., & Sheldon, K. M. (2011). A longitudinal experimental study comparing the effectiveness of happiness-enhancing strategies in Anglo Americans and Asian Americans. *Cognition & Emotion, 25,* 1263-1272.

Boehm, J. K., & Lyubomirsky, S. (2008). Does happiness lead to career success? *Journal of Career Assessment, 16,* 101-116.

Boniwell, I. (2006) Positive psychology in a nutshell. Berkshire: Open University Press.

Burns, A. B., Brown, J. S., Sachs-Ericsson, N., Plant, E. A., Curtis, J. T., Fredrickson, B. L., & Joiner, T. E., Jr. (2008). Upward spirals of positive emotion and coping: Replication, extension, and initial exploration of neurochemical substrates. *Personality and Individual Differences, 44,* 360-370.

Cameron , K. M. & Spreitzer, G. M. (2012). The Oxford handbook of positive organizational scholarship. New York: Oxford University Press.

Cohn, M. A. & Fredrickson, B. L. (2006). Beyond the moment, beyond the self: Shared ground between selective investment theory and the broaden-and-build theory of positive emotion. *Psychological Inquiry,* 39-44.

Csikszentmihalyi, M. (2008). Flow: The psychology of optimal experience. New York: HarperCollins Publishers.

Dambrun M., Ricard M., Després G., Drelon E., Gibelin E., Gibelin M., Loubeyre M., Py D., Delpy A., Garibbo C., Bray E., Lac G. & Michaux O. (2012) Measuring happiness: From fluctuating happiness to authentic–durable happiness. Front. *Psychology 3:16.* doi: 10.3389/fpsyg.2012.00016

David, S., Boniwell, I. & Conley Ayers, A. (2013). The Oxford handbook of happiness. New York: Oxford University Press.

Dutton, J. E., Quinn, R. E., & Cameron, K. (2003). Positive organizational scholarship: foundations of a new discipline. San Francisco: Berrett-Koehler Publishers.

Fowler, James H. & Christakis, Nicholas A. 2008. Dynamic spread of happiness in a large social network: Longitudinal analysis over 20 years in the Framingham Heart Study. *British Medical Journal 337*, no. a2338: 1-9

Fredrickson, B. L. (2009). Positivity: Top-notch research reveals the upward spiral that will change your life. New York: Crown Publishers.

Fredrickson, B. L., Cohn, M. A., Coffey, K. A., Pek, J., & Finkel, S. M. (2008). Open hearts build lives: Positive emotions, induced through loving-kindness meditation, build consequential personal resources. *Journal of Personality and Social Psychology*, 95(5): 1045–1062.

Fredrickson, B. L., & Branigan, C. (2005). Positive emotions broaden the scope of attention and thought-action repertoires. *Cognition and Emotion, 19*, 313-332.

Fredrickson, B. L., & Losada, M. (2005). Positive emotions and the complex dynamics of human flourishing. *American Psychologist, 60*, 678-686.

Fredrickson, B. L. (2004). The broaden-and-build theory of positive emotions. *Philosophical Transactions: Biological Sciences (The Royal Society of London) 359*, 1367- 1377.

Fredrickson, B. L. (2003). The value of positive emotions. *American Scientist, 91*, 330-335.

Fredrickson, B. L., & Joiner, T. (2002). Positive emotions trigger upward spirals toward emotional well-being. *Psychological Science, 13*, 172-175.

Fredrickson, B. L. (2001). The role of positive emotions in positive psychology: The broaden-and-build theory of positive emotions. *American Psychologist, 56*, 218-226.

Howell, R. T., Kern, M. L., & Lyubomirsky, S. (2007). Health benefits: Meta-analytically determining the impact of well-being on objective health outcomes. *Health Psychology Review, 1*, 83-136.

Huffman, J. C., Mastromauro, C. A., Boehm, J., Seabrook, R., Fricchione, G. L., Denninger, J. W., & Lyubomirsky, S. (2011). Development of a positive psychology intervention for patients with acute cardiovascular disease. *Heart International, 6*, 47-54.

Layous, K., Chancellor, J., Lyubomirsky, S., Wang, L., & Doraiswamy, P. M. (2011). Delivering happiness: Translating positive psychology intervention research for treating major and minor depressive disorders. *Journal of Alternative and Complementary Medicine, 17*, 675-683.

Lopez, S. J. & Snyder C. R. (2011). The Oxford handbook of positive psychology. New York: Oxford University Press.

Lyubomirsky, S. (2008). The how of happiness: A scientific approach to getting the life you want. New York: Penguin Press.

Lyubomirsky, S. (2014). The myths of happiness: What should make you happy, but doesn't, what shouldn't make you happy, but does. New York: Penguin Books.

Lyubomirsky, S., King, L. A., & Diener, E. (2005). The benefits of frequent positive affect: Does happiness lead to success? *Psychological Bulletin, 131*, 803-855.

Lyubomirsky, S., & Lepper, H. S. (1999). A measure of subjective happiness: Preliminary reliability and construct validation. *Social Indicators Research, 46*, 137-155.

Lyubomirsky, S. (2001). Why are some people happier than others?: The role of cognitive and motivational processes in well-being. *American Psychologist, 56*, 239-249.

Lyubomirsky, S., Boehm, J. K., Kasri, F., & Zehm, K. (2011). The cognitive and hedonic costs of dwelling on achievement-related negative experiences: Implications for enduring happiness and unhappiness. *Emotion, 11*, 1152-1167.

Lyubomirsky, S., & Boehm, J. K. (2010). Human motives, happiness, and the puzzle of parenthood: Commentary on Kenrick et al. (2010). *Perspectives on Psychological Science, 5*, 327-334.

Lyubomirsky, S., Dickerhoof, R., Boehm, J. K., & Sheldon, K. M. (2011). Becoming happier takes both a will and a proper way: An experimental longitudinal intervention to boost well-being. *Emotion, 11*, 391-402.

Orem, S. L., Binkert, J., & Clancy, A. L. (2007). Appreciative coaching: A positive process for change. San Francisco: Jossey-Bass.

Otake, K., Shimai, S., Tanaka-Matsumi, J., Otsui, K, & Fredrickson, B. L. (2006). Happy people become happier through kindness: A counting kindnesses intervention. *Journal of Happiness Studies, 7*, 361-375.

Parks, A., Della Porta, M., Pierce, R. S., Zilca, R. & Lyubomirsky, S. (2012). Pursuing happiness in everyday life: The characteristics and behaviors of online happiness seekers. *Emotion, 12(6)*, 1222-34.

Peterson, C. & Seligman, M. E. P. (2004). Character strengths and virtues: A handbook and classification. New York: Oxford University Press.

Ryan, R.M., Bernstein, J.H., & Brown, K.W. (2010). Weekends, work, and well-being: Psychological need satisfactions and day of the week effects on mood, vitality, and physical symptoms. *Journal of Social and Clinical Psychology, 29*, 95-122.

Ryan, R.M., Huta, V., & Deci, E.L. (2008). Living well: A self-determination theory perspective on eudaimonia. *Journal of Happiness Studies, 9*, 139-170.

Schwartz, B., Ward, A. H., Monterosso, J., Lyubomirsky, S., White, K., & Lehman, D. (2002). Maximizing versus satisficing: Happiness is a matter of choice. Journal of Personality and *Social Psychology, 83*, 1178-1197 .

Seligman, M. E. P. (2004) Authentic happiness: Using the new positive psychology to realize your potential for lasting fulfillment. New York: Free Press.

Seligman, M. E. P. (2012) Flourish: A visionary new understanding of happiness and well-being. New York: Free Press.

Sheldon, K. M., & Lyubomirsky, S. (2012). The challenge of staying happier: Testing the Hedonic Adaptation Prevention (HAP) model. *Personality and Social Psychology Bulletin, 38(5)*, 670-80.

Sheldon, K. M., Abad, N., Ferguson, Y., Gunz, A., Houser-Marko, L., Nichols, C. P., & Lyubomirsky, S. (2010). Persistent pursuit of need-satisfying goals leads to increased happiness: A 6-month experimental longitudinal study. *Motivation and Emotion, 34,* 39-48.

Sheldon, K. M., & Lyubomirsky, S. (2007). Is it possible to become happier? (And, if so, how?). *Social and Personality Psychology Compass, 1,* 129-145.

Sheldon, K. M., & Lyubomirsky, S. (2006a). How to increase and sustain positive emotion: The effects of expressing gratitude and visualizing best possible selves. *The Journal of Positive Psychology, 1,* 73-82.

Sheldon, K. M., & Lyubomirsky, S. (2006b). Achieving sustainable gains in happiness: Change your actions, not your circumstances. *Journal of Happiness Studies, 7,* 55-86.

Shimai, S., Otake, K., Utsuki, N., Ikemi, A., & Lyubomirsky, S. (2004). Development of a Japanese version of the Subjective Happiness Scale (SHS), and examination of its validity and reliability. *Japanese Journal of Public Health, 51,* 845-853.

Sin, N. L., & Lyubomirsky, S. (2009). Enhancing well-being and alleviating depressive symptoms with positive psychology interventions: A practice-friendly meta-analysis. *Journal of Clinical Psychology: In Session, 65,* 467-487.

Tkach, C., & Lyubomirsky, S. (2006). How do people pursue happiness? Relating personality, happiness-increasing strategies, and well-being. *Journal of Happiness Studies, 7,* 183-225.

Tugade, M. M. & Fredrickson, B. L. (2004). Resilient individuals use positive emotions to bounce back from negative emotional experiences. *Journal of Personality and Social Psychology, 86,* 320-333.

Tugade, M. M., Fredrickson, B. L., & Feldman Barrett, L. (2004). Psychological resilience and positive emotional granularity: Examining the benefits of positive emotions on coping and health. *Journal of Personality, 72,* 1161-1190.

ABOUT THE AUTHOR

In 1996, Dr. Aymee Coget (pronounced Co jjayy) made the decision to devote her entire life to helping millions of people live happier lives. After receiving her Ph.D. in Organizational Psychology with an emphasis in leadership and the science of happiness, she established an international consultancy, Happiness for HumanKind, based in San Francisco. The positive leadership programs teach individuals, relationships, families, groups, and businesses.

Dr. Aymee takes a 'training' approach with her students by seeing them as whole individuals who can learn to employ the skills of happiness science. She has over twenty years of experience in positive psychology and educates people on how to be sustainably happy as well as handle life's toughest challenges namely through her leadership training program, The Happiness Makeover®.

Dr. Aymee's combinations of techniques focusing on the mind, body, and spirit have helped people achieve a deep inner contentment that lasts regardless of life's situations. She teaches happiness with an applied, systematic formula which provides clear, consistent results.

She has received accolades for her work from international media and people who thought they would never experience happiness as demonstrated in client testimonials. Being recognized as a leader in helping others feel better, Dr. Aymee has blogged for many websites including Yahoo! Health and Blogher. She consults with global companies on sustainable happiness from perspectives of products, customers, employees, media, policy, and technology.

She is a Happiness Content Provider for magazines, newspapers, and television in which she frequently comments on the topics of sustainable happiness, resiliency, global education, and well-being technology. She advises software companies on how to benefit humankind.

In March of 2020, Dr. Aymee was a member of the working group for the recommended practice that assesses the impact of autonomous and intelligent systems on human well-being put forth by the *IEEE P7010*.

To learn more about her programs and additional resources, visit www.HappinessforHumanKind.com

Also by Dr. Aymee Coget: *Find Your Blissful Calling*

APPENDIX A

Happiness Makeover® Protocol Daily Accountability Sheet

THE HAPPINESS MAKEOVER PROTOCOL	Date / /	Date / /	Date / /	Date / /	Date / /	Date / /	Date / /
Morning Routine							
Wake up and Smile							
Today is the happiest day of my life!							
Go to the bathroom and brush teeth 5 Duchenne smile push ups							
Laughter practice and 5 I am happy jumps							
Sing zippity doo da (or another happy song							
Gratitude practice (walk, jog, drive, shower, journal)							
Ask Heart, "Where am I on the happiness scale and what do I need to be a 10? Anything else?"							
Isagenix							
Daytime Routine							
5 acts of kindness							
Positive language (eliminate no, not, dont, cant, should, but, try)							
Inner colleague creation (switch every negative thought to a positive)							
Live in the moment (how many times did you do the 5 steps?)							
At least 20 minutes of exercise (includes walking)							
Happiness boosts							
Sleep Routine							
Recount 5 acts of kindness							
Ask yourself "What are 3 good things that happened and how did I contribute to them?"							
Read to yourself inner colleague creation thoughts from the day							
Reiki							
Happiness Challenges							
Happiness Shield(KLOGZ: kindness, love, optimism, gratitude, zest)							
Live in the moment - 5 steps 100x							
Acceptance model(DAPAG:decide, accept, practical, ask, gratitude)							
Letting go / Filling up							
Your strengths							
Faith							
Ask heart							
AAA (Admiration, Appreciation, Affections)							
Inner colleague creation (switch negative thought to positive)							

APPENDIX B

48 BARRIERS TO AUTHENTICITY

Barriers to authenticity can occur when...

SELF:

- There are hidden parts of the self and prevalence of unconscious thought. (Harter, 2002)
- Belief that the self is a mechanistic character with rationality as the essence of humanity. (Gergen, 1991; Bugantal, 1965)
- Imposter tendencies represent the need for narcissistic enhancement as a defense against core feelings of worthlessness. (Deutsch, 1955; Kohut, 1984)
- If the child accepts falsification of information or experience it may lead to the falsification of the self. (Harter, 1997)
- If the child displays behavior that meets the needs of someone else, then there is risk of alienating the inner experiences of the true self. (Crittenden, 1994; Stern, 1985; Winnicott, 1965)
- Multiple selves are created to adapt in multiple social roles and contexts. (Erickson, 1950; Griffen, Shassin, & Young, 1981; Harter & Monsour, 1992; Kolligian, 1990; Smollnar & Youniss, 1985; Gergen, 1991)
- Lack of awareness of multiple selves. (Gergen, 1991)
- There is judgment of self from meeting outside expectations. (Horney, 1950)
- The personal self is crafted through the linguistic exchanges of others and the incorporation of attitudes that significant others appear to hold about one's self. (Harter, 1997)
- High self monitors will suppress the true self in order to gain approval from others. (Snyder, 1987)

SOCIALLY CONDITIONED:

- The internal experience of authenticity does not match with dominant culture. (Horney, 1950)
- When people need to win the acceptance of others. (Goffman, 1959)
- Outer directed individuals become malleable to social demands. (Riesman, 1950).

- When vocabulary linked to deception is used. Adjectives include elusive, evasive, wily, phony, artificial, two-faced, manipulative, calculating, pretentious, crafty, conniving, duplicitous, deceitful, dishonest. Nouns include hypocrite, charlatan, chameleon, imposter, fake and fraud. Verbs include fabricating, withholding, concealing, distorting, falsifying, pulling the wool over someone's eyes, posturing, charading, faking, and hiding behind a façade. (Lerner, 1993)
- Language can drive a wedge between two simultaneous forms of interpersonal experience: as it is lived and as it is verbally represented. The capacity for objectifying the self through language allows one to transcend and therefore potentially distort immediate experience. (Stern, 1985)
- The tactical flexibility of the protean self in uncertain conditions. (Lifton, 1993)

GENDER:

- Women focus on others instead of self. (Miller, 1976)
- American women lose their voice in adolescence. (Gilligan, Lyons, & Hanmer, 1989)
- Women were taught to be subordinate and subordination and leadership are incompatible. (Miller, 1976)
- Women embody characteristics of the good woman stereotype. (Gilligan et al, 1989)
- A woman who relates to feminine orientation. (Gilligan et al, 1989; Lerner, 1993)
- Women experience a lack of awareness about their "assumptions of knowing" which make up the thought process. Women adopt a man's way of knowing. (Lyons, 1996)
- Women suppress thoughts and opinions, which leads to "loss of voice". Especially problematic for adolescent girls. (Gilligan, 1982; Gilligan, Lyons, & Hammer, 1989)
- There is an overemphasis on connectedness and caregiving. (Chodorow, 1978; Gilligan, 1982; Jordon, 1991; Miller, 1986)
- Women are fearful that if they act on their own needs and desires, it would threaten their existing relationships. (Gilligan, 1982; Gilligan et al, 1989; Jordon, Kaplan, Miller, Stiver, & Striver, 1991; Lerner, 1993)
- The dominant culture has assumptions against women in leadership. (Eagly, 2005)

FOLLOWERSHIP:

- Perceptions of followers are not inline with the true self of the leader. (Eagly, 2005)
- There is a contextual situational agreement between followers and the leader. (Goffman, 1959)
- Followers are inauthentic. (Goffman, 1959)
- There is value incongruence between leader and followership. (Avolio, 2004)
- One is being phony and not stating a true opinion by saying what others want to hear. (Harter et al, 1996)

SPIRITUAL:

- The dominant culture has assumptions against women in leadership. (Eagly, 2005)
- A person engages in Ich (I) - E (object) relationships because there is an absence of God. (Buber, 1970)
- Someone does not embrace the human sense of spirit – daimon. (Aristotle, n.d.)

PROFESSIONAL:

- A person does not have meaning in their professional life. (Frankl, 1963)

DEVELOPMENTAL:

- A child does not have an environment where language, support, and acceptance occur to differentiate true versus false self. (Harter, 2002)
- Caregivers did not validate the child's true self. (Bleiberg, 1984)
- When parents are over involved with their infant; the infant develops a false self based on compliance. (Winnicott, 1965)
- Adolescents use Normative role experimentation when one tries on different personas. (Broughton, 1981; Selman, 1980)
- Adolescents obscure their true self when they become aware they are targets of others judgment. (Elkind, 1967)
- There is misrepresentation of a child's actual experience in their narrative because it is heavily influenced by the parent's emphasis on particular events deemed important to them and not the child. (Bowlby, 1980; Bretherton, 1991; Crittenden, 1994)
- Children experience direct or indirect messages from the parents that certain events may be left untold or forgotten. (Dunn, Brown, & Beardsall, 1991)

- Abuse occurs by caregivers or the child experiences lack of attunement to their needs, failure of empathy, lack of validation, threats of harm, coercion, and enforced compliance. (Bleiberg, 1984; Stern, 1985; Winnicott, 1965)
- Sexual and physical abuse with family members causes the child to split off experiences relegating them to a private self or inaccessible self. (Harter, 1997)
- A conscious pathway is developed, in that the abused child comes to see the true self as corroded with inner badness and as therefore to be concealed at all cost. (Herman, 1992)
- There is a childhood trauma of the loss of love. (Miller, 1976, 1986)
- Persistent attempts to be good, in order to please the parents, lead the child to develop a socially acceptable self that is experienced as false. (Harter, 1997)
- A false self will emerge to the extent that caregivers make their love contingent on the child's living up to their particular standards, since the child must adopt a socially implanted self. (Harter, 1997)
- Children experience "contingent self-esteem" where their self-esteem is dependent on receiving support for meeting externally imposed standards of parents and peers and may lead to further falsification of the self. (Harter, Marold, Whitesell, & Cobbs, 1996)

Made in the USA
Columbia, SC
29 October 2020